W9-BNA-702

INSTRUCTOR'S GUIDE

picturing texts

Cheryl E. Ball
Michigan Technological University

W. W. NORTON & COMPANY

New York London

W. W. Norton & Company has been independent since its founding in 1923, when William Warder Norton and Mary D. Herter Norton first published lectures delivered at the People's Institute, the adult education division of New York City's Cooper Union. The Nortons soon expanded their program beyond the Institute, publishing books by celebrated academics from America and abroad. By mid-century, the two major pillars of Norton's publishing program—trade books and college texts—were firmly established. In the 1950s, the Norton family transferred control of the company to its employees, and today—with a staff of four hundred and a comparable number of trade, college, and professional titles published each year—W. W. Norton & Company stands as the largest and oldest publishing house owned wholly by its employees.

Composition by PennSet, Inc.
Manufacturing by Courier Companies

ISBN 0-393-92507-2

W. W. Norton & Company, Inc., 500 Fifth Avenue, New York, N.Y. 10110-0017
<www.wwnorton.com>

W. W. Norton & Company Ltd., Castle House, 75/76 Wells Street, London W1T 3QT

1 2 3 4 5 6 7 8 9 0

contents

4 Representing Others   *58*

5 Constructing Realities   *77*

6   Picturing Argument   *93*

7   Designing Texts   *104*

preface
to the instructor's guide

Picturing Texts by Lester Faigley, Diana George, Anna Palchik, and Cynthia Selfe is based on the premises that students are becoming increasingly sophisticated consumers and critics of visual texts and that our classrooms must shift to accommodate these visual literacies, including both the reading of visuals and the production of visual texts. *Picturing Texts* offers a rhetorical framework for studying texts composed of both words and images, along with key terms for helping students understand how texts work the way they do, and guidelines to help them read and design texts effectively. By examining and producing texts—verbal, visual, and multimodal—students will begin to understand how to read, interpret, compose, and design such texts themselves.

Picturing Texts offers three strategies to help students expand their notions of composing verbal and visual texts—writing *about* visuals, writing *with* visuals, and writing that *is* visual.

The first strategy is to read and write *about* visual texts. Thinking critically and writing about texts helps ground students in the rhetorical choices that writers and designers make. In Chapter 2, "Looking Closer," students are asked to look at two pictures. The first is the September 11, 2001, photo taken by Thomas Franklin of firefighters raising the American flag amidst the rubble of the World Trade Center. The second is the 1945 photo taken by Joe Rosenthal of three Marines raising the American flag in Iwo Jima. Throughout the chapter, students are shown how to look at these two photos rhetorically. The chapter includes a set of questions to guide students through the process of critically reading a visual text along with tips for writing up an analysis of those texts based on their understanding of audience, genre, visual composition strategies, and historical context.

The second strategy is to compose *with* visuals. In Chapter 6, "Picturing Argument," which discusses how images can be read persuasively, one assignment asks students to examine greeting cards to see how the images chosen by the designer try to portray a particular feeling or event. Based on their analyses of some sample greeting cards, they are then asked to create their own cards, relying mostly on images to portray a holiday of their choice. Then they are asked to workshop the design and revise it based on peer comments, and to write a design justification for the choices they made. Writing about what they have tried to produce themselves gives students increased awareness of the rhetorical choices required in visual as well as verbal texts.

Finally, students learn how to *make* their writing visual—that is, how to design written text. Chapter 7, "Designing Texts," shows the example of how one student first recast an article as a brochure to reach her audience better and then worked to revise the brochure's design to improve its rhetorical effectiveness. In Chapter 4, "Representing Others," students are asked, after reading primary source materials, about how to create comic book stereotypes, and to try to design their own comic book characters *without* stereotypical features. Then they are asked to get feedback from classmates on their design and to write a persuasive letter to comic book publishers convincing them that using characters without stereotypical features would be of interest to their target readers.

If visual rhetoric has been primarily regarded by composition instructors as choosing fonts and placing elements on a page, *Picturing Texts* wants to expand it to include the many visual ways texts make arguments. In expanding the notion of composition to include the design of texts that incorporate more than the written word, you can engage students with a broad range of cultural texts—print advertisements, scrapbooks, brochures, flyers, commercials, photographs, documentaries, Web sites, films— as well as essays, memoirs, even stories and poems. Reading and discussing these multimodal genres provides a rhetorical foundation for understanding them, and having students design multimodal texts offers an in-depth process for putting their genre knowledge and design ideas into practice.

With the increasing access that students have to technology, the possibility of producing multimodal texts has migrated from the realm of graphic designers and specialists to that of everyday people. On the same computers and with the same software that students word-process an essay, they can choose fonts and try out various layout techniques to create sophisticated texts. Even without access to technology, they can explore design concepts with the lower-technology alternatives on which software programs are based—cutting and pasting works in any medium. The authors of *Picturing Texts* believe that introducing composition students to the processes of design will help them to become more effective communicators, and we hope and expect that they will have some fun in the process.

How *Picturing Texts* Is Structured

Picturing Texts is designed to have students move from reading texts ("Looking Closer") to producing texts. Students start with experiences they are familiar with and work outward, thinking about and incorporating experiences that may not be as close to their own—moving from texts that are basically "personal" in Chapter 3 ("Making Lives Visible") to writing about others in Chapter 4 ("Representing Others") and constructing arguments in Chapter 6 ("Picturing Argument"). Along the way, students will be reading, writing, and designing texts that represent each of these chapters' main points. The final chapter, "Designing Texts," can be used at any point, as it introduces many of the design practices students will use in their own texts and in the assignments for each chapter. We hope that structuring the textbook this way will help students move from personal experience to argument, and from being critical readers of visual and verbal texts to becoming effective composers of such texts.

How to Use the Features in Each Chapter

Each chapter opens with an introduction, followed by readings and assignments. You'll find two features in each chapter introduction that will prompt students to think briefly about some of the principles of the chapter. Snapshot exercises ask them to think about some familiar photos (such as pictures they've taken of friends) as texts, leading them to consider how they make lives visible, construct a certain reality, and so on. Image Conscious prompts are very brief exercises asking students to pay attention to other visual texts, including ones found in magazines, newspapers, online, and elsewhere. These exercises can serve as brief homework or journal assignments or as discussion prompts in class.

Another feature is the Gallery of Images at the end of each chapter. The gallery sections offer multiple images for students to peruse. Each one has a brief caption giving some information about the artist and the composition of the image, and this manual offers some short questions to get students thinking more about the immediate and broader contexts of each image. You might wish to use these questions as assignments, perhaps asking students to write a response to an image of their choice. These images are a great way to start class discussion. Another way to use the galleries is as a starting point for each chapter. For instance, you could explore the gallery images in class before any chapter reading is assigned, prompting students to think about what they think the images "say"—perhaps a good way to get them thinking about what the chapter will cover. You may also find it useful to refer students to the galleries when examples of visual texts are needed for assignments. And you can have students do further research on an artist or genre based on the gallery images.

Each chapter includes readings, with study questions and writing assignments. You'll find two kinds of exercises—Focus and Respond—each with two to three questions. The Focus section asks students to look closely at the text they just read and to respond to short discussion-based questions. The Focus questions are good to use to start discussion in class about the readings (although a few of them may require time outside class to complete). The Respond questions offer more extensive assignments—finding other similar texts, researching ideas discussed in the reading, and writing and designing texts.

Following the readings is a larger assignment called Picture This that brings together, usually in several steps, all of the ideas covered in the chapter. A typical Picture This assignment will ask students to research, collect texts, analyze texts, write and design their own texts, and perhaps present their work to the class. The assignments in Picture This make ideal team or whole-class projects.

Another very important feature of *Picturing Texts* is the Web site, at <www.picturingtexts.com>. Throughout the Instructor's Guide, we will point you to places on the site where you can find further resources, including URLs that pertain to particular assignments. The Web site also features tips for doing research on the Web and contains several exercises and further readings for each chapter, focusing specifically on Web-based texts, including animated texts and some texts that contain sound.

How to Use the Guide

This guide parallels the structure of *Picturing Texts*, each chapter corresponding to a chapter in the book. We offer possible answers and, more often, suggestions for how to approach, discuss, and help students achieve a better level of understanding for each of the Focus and Respond questions.

We do not offer exact answers in most cases because, as *Picturing Texts* demonstrates, any reader's understanding of a text will depend on many factors, including his or her immediate context as well as the context in which the text was originally composed. We do, however, try to lead you to some possible answers through questions (sometimes answered within parenthetical statements following those questions). Our main goal is to help you and your students see the multiple possibilities and meanings that can be created through the use of visual and verbal texts. Although this does not mean that texts can be read any way one wants, as with any text, there are usually several rhetorical (thus, probable) ways of reading visual texts. Our suggestions and possible answers encourage you to explore these varying meanings yourself and with your class. Unlike instruction in which students are "given" answers, the pedagogy behind this textbook and guides focuses more on collaborative (student and teacher) learning and exploration of possibilities, which, we hope will lead students to be better critical thinkers and composers of texts.

Planning Your Syllabus

We encourage you to use *Picturing Texts* to suit your own needs. You may decide not to use every chapter or not to follow the order of the chapters, and the textbook can easily be used in many different ways. One way to use the book is in linear order, with the exception of Chapter 7, "Designing Texts," which you might wish to use after Chapter 1. We assume that "Designing Texts" will be referred to as a resource for students when thinking about their own designs or for your evaluation of their designs.

The pedagogical focus of each chapter is described below, along with three possible ways of using these chapters.

- Chapter 1 outlines useful vocabulary for discussing texts and design.

- Chapter 2 focuses broadly on how to read a text that is designed with images, graphics, words, or any combination of these things.

- Chapter 3 covers some personal texts, showing how writers can use words, images, and design to make their lives visible.

- Chapter 4 expands the focus beyond students' personal experience to texts that represent others.

- Chapter 5 shows that images and other texts are not transparent windows—that they always construct (or mediate) what they represent.

- Chapter 6 focuses on how to form an argument using a designed text.

- Chapter 7 outlines design principles that are useful for creating texts.

Three Syllabi

1. From Understanding Texts to Producing Texts for Others

Chapter 1: vocabulary

Chapter 2: reading and analysis

Chapter 7: design principles

Chapter 3: personal texts

Chapter 6: visual arguments

Chapter 4: texts that represent others

Chapter 5: ethics and constructing texts

2. A Civic Advocacy Approach
(using ethics to build complex visual arguments)

Chapter 1: vocabulary

Chapter 7: design principles

Chapter 2: reading and analysis

Chapter 5: ethics and constructing texts

Chapter 3: personal texts

Chapter 4: texts that represent others

Chapter 6: visual arguments

3. Designing Texts

Chapter 7: design principles

Chapter 3: personal texts

Chapter 4: texts that represent others

Chapter 5: the ethics of constructing texts

Chapter 6: visual arguments

Recommended Readings

Bolter, Jay David, and Richard Grusin. *Remediation: Understanding New Media.* Cambridge: MIT P, 2000.

Faigley, Lester. "Material Literacy and Visual Design." *Rhetorical Bodies.* Ed. Jack Selzer and Sharon Crowley. U of Wisconsin P, 1999.

George, Diana. "From Analysis to Design: Visual Communication in the Teaching of Writing." *College Composition and Communication* 54.1 (Sept. 2002): 11–39.

George, Diana, and Diane Shoos. "Dropping Bread Crumbs in the Intertextual Forest: Critical Literacy in a Postmodern Age." *Passions, Pedagogies, and 21st Century Technologies.* Ed. Gail Hawisher and Cynthia Selfe. Logan: Utah State UP, 1999.

Heller, Steven, and Karen Pomeroy. *Design Literacy: Understanding Graphic Design.* New York: Allworth, 1997.

Kress, Günther. "Multimodality." *Multiliteracies: Literacy Learning and the Design of Social Futures*. Ed. Bill Cope and Mary Kalantzis. New York: Routledge, 1999.

Kress, Günther, and Theo van Leeuwen. *Reading Images: The Grammar of Visual Design*. New York: Routledge, 1996.

Kress, Günther, and Theo van Leeuwen. *Multimodal Discourse: The Modes and Media of Contemporary Communication*. New York: Oxford UP, 2001.

New London Group. *Multiliteracies: Literacy Learning and the Design of Social Futures*. Ed. Bill Cope and Mary Kalantzis. New York: Routledge, 2000.

Rasula, Jed, and Steve McCaffery. *Imagining Language: An Anthology*. Cambridge: MIT P, 2001.

Selfe, Cynthia. "Lest We Think the Revolution Is a Revolution: Images of Technology and the Nature of Change." *Passions, Pedagogies, and 21st Century Technologies*. Logan: Utah State UP, 1999.

Smith, Keith. *Text in the Book Format*. 2nd ed. Rochester, NY: Visual Studies Workshop P, 1995.

Trimbur, John, ed. *Popular Literacy: Studies in Cultural Practices and Poetics*. Pittsburgh Series in Composition, Literacy, and Culture. Pittsburgh: U of Pittsburgh P, 2001.

Williams, Robin. *The Non-designers Design Book*. 2nd ed. Atlanta: Peachpit, 2001.

Wysocki, Anne. "Impossibly Distinct: On Form/Content and Word/Image in Two Pieces of Computer-Based Interactive Multimedia." *Computers and Composition* 18.2 (2001): 137–62.

introduction

The introductory chapter of *Picturing Texts* starts with the discovery of the Chauvet cave paintings in 1994. These cave paintings signify that humans have long been image-making and image-reading creatures. This chapter briefly outlines the use of images in different cultures across the world and how we read those images, with and without the help of words. The chapter outlines three key concepts for reading visual and verbal texts, being aware of *immediate context*, *broader context*, and *intertextuality*.

The concept of *immediate context* allows readers to interpret texts with the main rhetorical principles in mind: audience and purpose. Knowing who designed a text, for whom it is intended, and its main purpose can help us to determine the immediate context for understanding a text. We understand the *broader context* of a text by knowing the social, historical, cultural, and economic forces that surrounded the creation of that text; because we are influenced daily by such forces, understanding how the broader context affects the design of a text will help us interpret it more fully. Finally, *intertextuality* requires us to acknowledge that a text can often refer to another text. Nearly all texts refer to and build on other texts, so understanding such intertextuality assumes that we are familiar with its precursors. In this way, a reader's personal knowledge will influence how he or she interprets a text. Chapter 2 offers a detailed reading of two images using contextual concepts, and all of these ideas will be further explored in chapter assignments.

1 picturing texts

This chapter discusses some basic approaches to understanding how to interpret visuals and the combination of words and images. Starting with the comparison of texts from the museums on the National Mall in Washington, D.C., we ask students to compare how each kind of communication (words, images, and the combination of both) helps to make meaning in a text. This textbook presents visuals and multimodal texts combining both verbal and graphic content as available for "reading" and provides students with several key concepts in this chapter to help them interpret various kinds of texts that they will encounter in and outside the classroom.

The chapter also touches on two common ways that words and visuals are often combined, and on how readers "see" texts through their own knowledge and experience.

- **Charts and Graphs: Explaining with Visuals** discusses how some concepts are easier to understand with a visual explanation, rather than with words alone.

- **Captions: Explaining Visuals with Words** discusses how words can add to visuals to make meaning.

- **What We See When Looking at a Text** discusses how each reader brings his or her own knowledge to interpret a text, and how different readers may read texts differently depending on their knowledge of the subject.

Snapshot

At the end of the chapter introduction, right before the readings, a short exercise invites students to find a snapshot and to write a caption for it. In doing so, they explore how words and images work together—how the snapshot makes meaning on its own, and how that meaning changes with the addition of an explanatory caption.

Exercises for Working with Key Terms

In exploring how snapshots make meaning, students might want to use the key terms that are explained in the chapter. Below are some possible in-class exercises to help students better understand these concepts.

Balance (see p. 26)

Balance (see p. 26)

Before class, photocopy the Levi's SilverTab jeans ad onto a transparency. Cut out the part of the ad with the round SilverTab logo and keep it. Show students the original ad in Chapter 1 as it appears on page 27 and then show them the transparency with the round logo gone. Ask them if the balance of the ad changes. They may say it feels a little unbalanced, favoring the top of the ad page—top-heavy, so to speak.

Next, place the SilverTab logo in the middle of the ad, over the boots. How do the students react to this new placement according to balance? They may say that the balance is still top-heavy or that the logo, in relation to the similarly sized Levi's logo, makes the ad seem balanced in the middle. (But then what about the abundance of white space at the bottom of the ad?)

Finally, place the SilverTab logo to the left of the page, in the white space between the tip of the boot and the calf of the person—directly across from the Levi's logo. How is the balance now? Are there other places where students may want to place the logo to achieve a different feeling of balance or unbalance? How do different positions affect the ad's meaning? Ask the students why they think the designer chose to put the SilverTab logo where she or he did. Perhaps the designer put it there because it balances the ad, or perhaps for a more specific reason—for example, the Levi's brand attempts to appear rugged and rough (also seen through the boots and spurs), and the cowboy's boots seem poised to crush the SilverTab logo.

Classification (see p. 28)

Before class, find several examples of Greek columns other than those pictured in the textbook. For example, search the Google image database (see <www.picturingtexts.com> for suggestions and tips to help students conduct their own online search) by typing in "Greek columns" (with quotation marks for more accurate results). You can also find books in the library or look in travel magazines. Get at least five or six examples of Greek columns from several different genres—for example, line drawings, photographs, and sketches. Photocopy or make transparencies of all examples, making sure to put only one kind of column on each piece of paper or overhead.

In class, ask students to write words that describe the architectural elements of each of the Greek columns that appear in *Picturing Texts*. (Have them work in groups on this assignment, splitting the class into three groups—one for each type of column—or have each group describe all three of the columns, thus getting more descriptions.) After they have written a list of words for the columns, show the students the other kinds of columns you have collected and ask them to classify them according to the descriptions they have written.

You may also use this exercise to introduce visual *genres*. After they have classified the columns using words, have students reclassify all of the columns according to visual genres—photos, sketches, drawings—and have them write observations about each genre. Do drawings work better for showing detail than photos? What can you show with a photo that you cannot with a painting? And so on.

Comparison and Contrast (see p. 30)

In class, have students look at the Margaret Bourke-White photo *At the Time of the Louisville Flood* that appears on page 31. In this photo are several thematic contrasts that can be explored to help students understand comparison and contrast.

On the chalkboard, write a list of the visual elements in the photo. (Alternatively, make a photocopy with a transparency of this image and circle the elements with an overhead pen.) There are four main elements to compare in this photo: 1. "World's Highest Standard of Living," 2. "There's no way like the American Way," 3. the billboard/mural of the smiling family and dog in the automobile, and 4. the line of people standing on the sidewalk. Start by asking students what each element means to them. Explain that the line of people is a breadline; the caption provides context for this analysis.

Once all four elements have been discussed, ask students how they contrast with one another and how the contrasts affect what the photo "says." The idea of the well-off, happy family and the text stating that being well-to-do is patriotic on the background billboard sharply contrast with the Louisville citizens who are obviously not well off after the flood.

Description (see p. 32)

Ask students to name all of the details they see in the Walker Evans photo of the general store on page 33. Write them on the board or an overhead. Are any details missed? How would students describe the store to a person who is blind?

Alternatively, ask students to look around the classroom and to describe all of the details of the room that they see. Ask them what they notice now that they may not have noticed before doing this exercise.

Emphasis (see p. 34)

Before class, make an enlarged transparency of the middle page (THREAT, HOPE, CHALLENGE) of *World Tour* magazine on page 34.

In class, show students the larger version of the page you have photocopied and ask them what they first notice on the page. Then, ask them the second thing they noticed. Most students will probably say THREAT and HOPE. Discuss with the class why these are the first two elements they notice on the page. Perhaps it is because THREAT is near the top of the page—a place of high priority in visual design, thus carrying much emphasis. Because Western readers understand texts from left to right and top to bottom, we approach this page from the top first; THREAT is the first large element we encounter.

Next, ask students if they noticed the black bar of masthead materials on the left side of the page. If any students noticed this first, ask them if they read the text before noticing other elements on the page. If not, perhaps it is because of the size of the smaller, masthead text in relation to the largest text on the page—again, THREAT. In this ad, the designer wanted the word THREAT to appear first and most prominently. Ask students if they can hypothesize why. (Without reading the smaller print, it would be hard to say for sure, but they may come up with interesting theories.)

Metaphor (see p. 36)

(see p. 36)

In the American Cancer Society ad on page 37, the metaphor is a smoking cigarette as a sure way to kill yourself—as sure as shooting yourself with a gun. Ask students to determine the nature of the metaphor based on the elements in the ad (and what they know about the agenda of the American Cancer Society). Further issues to discuss might include 1. why the designer chose a gun and not some other object to get at a similar meaning, 2. what effects seeing a gun has on the audience, 3. what effect it would have on the purpose of the ad if the designer had substituted another object (thus changing the metaphor) such as a machine gun (is it typical for people to kill themselves with machine guns?) or something totally different such as a water pistol.

Narration (see p. 38)

(see p. 38)

Before class, make a transparency of the stills from an early motion picture on page 39.

In class, cover the last two stills in the sequence and ask students to determine what action is taking place. Do the same for each of the other two stills. Then, show students all three stills and ask them to describe what action they think is taking place in this scene. (They will typically say dancing, but some may say fighting. If there are differences of opinion, this is a good way to explore why trying to determine narrative from images that have no accompanying text presents difficulties such as varied interpretations based on the audience's understanding of the scene.) Discuss whether their interpretation of the individual stills differs from their understanding of all three stills seen in sequence, and if so, how. Ask what helped them to understand what the scene was about, even if they thought that the individual stills presented a different narrative.

Additionally, you may want students to explore further how narrative in images is constructed. After doing the above exercise, ask students to look at Picasso's *Guernica* on page 39, and to sketch out how they might represent that painting as a series of still images—in effect, creating a storyboard or set of film cells that they can read sequentially to show the narrative of *Guernica* in a different manner. Students can trace parts of the painting onto paper (bring some tracing paper for them). Ask them to frame specific images within the painting to show how a sequence of events in *Guernica* occurs.

Pattern *(see p. 40)*

Before class, make a transparency of the Wrangler Jeans ad on page 40. Cut a piece of paper so that when you lay it over the ad, only one square inch of the leaves shows.

In class, show students the transparency with only the square inch of leaves showing. Ask them to identify the pattern and what they think the larger image consists of. Discuss how elements within the small section of leaves help them to identify what they are seeing. For instance, several elements—sunlight, the shadows of the leaves, and the angle of the tree bark—all indicate that there is a tree that has lots of leaves. And since students cannot see beyond the tree and leaves to a contrasting background, they may surmise that there is more than one tree—so a small forest would be the likely scenery based on the small square of pattern you have provided.

Point of View *(see p. 42)*

In class, ask students to look at the photograph *Afghanistan,* an image on page 43 of a woman walking down the street. Ask students to identify what seems odd about the image—that the two pairs of feet seem to be dangling as if kids are walking in midair. Ask how the perspective the photographer chose creates an unbalanced feeling in the photo. Next, ask what the photographer did to help the audience understand the oddities of this photo. Discuss how the point of view of the photographer, reflected in his choosing to include the shadow of the cannon, affects the statement the photo makes.

Proportion *(see p. 44)*

Bring to class an almanac or other reference book that would contain the height of the Eiffel Tower. (Or use the Internet if you're in a networked classroom.) Using the photograph *Paris* that appears on page 45 as a reference point, ask students to find the height of the Eiffel Tower. Then, ask them what the height of the man in the background might be. Based on those numbers, ask students to estimate what the height of the woman might be, if the elements of the picture were actually to proportion. Discuss with students why they think the photographer chose to place the elements in such dis-proportion to each other. Ask what the point of the photograph seems to be. Perhaps the photographer wanted to emphasize the role of women in French society. Remind the students that the photographer is a man. Perhaps the photo says something about *his* perspective on the important aspects of French culture. Can students come up with other ideas?

Next, ask students to draw their own versions of this photograph in which all of the elements are in proportion to each other. How do their versions differ in purpose from the photographer's version?

Unity *(see p. 46)*

For this exercise, students can work in groups. Bring several blank transparencies and some overhead markers for groups to use (one for each group).

In class, ask students to look at the *Hot Shot Eastbound* photograph on page 47. Ask them to describe the different elements they see in the photo. These might include the foreground image of the man in the convertible, the line of cars in the middle of the photo, the passing train, and the image of the airplane on the drive-in screen. Ask students what elements are repeated (the parked cars in the middle, the dirt path in front of the convertible, the dirt mound on the railroad tracks, the pole of the drive-in screen, and the telephone/electric pole next to the tracks, etc.). How does such repetition affect the way we see the photo? Do we view these elements individually or as groups? How does repetition of similar elements create unity in the photo?

Next, ask students to form groups and give each group a blank transparency and marker. Ask them to place the transparency over the photo in the textbook and to draw the photographer's invisible grid, using as many horizontal and vertical lines as they need. They might want to refer to the unifying elements discussed above as starting points for finding the invisible grid. (Students may need extra transparencies, in case they have to start over.) Discuss the different grids each group draws and how complex the grids are. When they draw the grids, do they notice more repeated elements? Why do they think the photographer chose to shoot a scene with so many elements? How do the elements and the grid draw the audience's attention in the photo? (The elements of the airplane, the train, and even the boy in the convertible seem to be moving toward the right of the photo— toward the east, perhaps, as the title indicates.)

MITCHELL STEPHENS, "By Means of the Visible"

This chapter from Mitchell Stephens's book *The Rise of the Image, the Fall of the Word* traces how television producers came to rely on visuals to make meaning, finding they could juxtapose more visuals in less space. He notes a similar shift toward visuals in the introduction of graphic user interfaces on computers, such as Apple's Macintosh and Microsoft's Windows operating systems, both of which use familiar icons to represent organizational and operational patterns. Stephens shows how people have historically been skeptical of images as a means of communication, believing that images do not carry as much meaning as words. He argues, however, that making meaning from visuals, including fast-cutting visuals such as in MTV videos or commercials, takes as much skill as reading written words and that visuals sometimes convey more information in less space than written words can.

Focus.

1. This exercise asks students to underline each passage in which Stephens presents a historical view that visuals misrepresent, distort, or devalue reality. Ask students to do this exercise as they read through the essay for the first time, or have them do it as a re-reading exercise in class. After they have underlined the passages they find that are "against" visuals, discuss how these complaints might be similar to those heard today about visuals.

Take this exercise one step further: Tape a fast-paced music video or a similarly edited commercial and show it in class. If you are in a computer-networked classroom, you can download videos from MTV.com. (You will need the RealOne player to view the videos, available for free download at <www.real.com>. See also the *Picturing Texts* Web site.) Quote Günther Kress, a theorist who studies the semiotics of visual texts, who once said, "Music videos have no narratives." Watch the video and ask students if they agree with Kress's comment. Do they find any narrative in the video? Given what Stephens says, do they think visuals convey less meaning than written words?

2. This exercise asks students to consider whether Stephens, who wrote about the power of visuals using mostly written text, could have made the same points in another medium. Point out that this book was published by Oxford University Press, in hardcover, in 1998. Ask students to determine, based on this information, the likely audience of Stephens's book. What do the publisher, format, and date tell us about who he is trying to convince? Students may readily see that visuals do convey meaning. Whom do they know who would need to be con-

vinced that visuals (and music videos) carry meaning? (Perhaps their parents?) Do they think the historical complaints that Stephens highlights are as strongly felt in the twenty-first century as they were when the book was first published?

Then have students explore whether Stephens's argument would have been better made through another medium—such as video. They may say yes, but remind them that they did not necessarily need convincing that visuals carry meaning; Stephens's intended audience would likely be less persuaded by watching a video than *reading* about it. Finally, ask students to brainstorm about how they might re-envision Stephens's essay as a video—how some of his main ideas might be represented visually.

Respond.

1. This exercise asks students to visit the Studio 10 Web site (see <www.picturingtexts.com>) and to write an essay with reference to Stephens's essay on whether these images of the Mona Lisa devalue the original painting or help us to see it in a new way. (To see a digital version of the original painting, visit the Louvre's Web site; there's a link at <www.picturingtexts.com>.)

   You may want to suggest that they read Walter Benjamin's essay "The Work of Art in the Age of Mechanical Reproduction," which can be found in many places online (See <www.picturingtexts.com> for exact URLs). Benjamin remarks on the lack of "aura" reproduced art has, arguing that a reproduction can never be as good as the original because the artwork has been taken out of the original context. You need only assign the Preface, since Benjamin touches on many of these ideas therein.

2. This exercise asks students to write an essay that considers what their lives would be like if they had constant access to the Internet with a wireless computer. Give students the option of writing a short story for this assignment—sometimes this creative genre allows students to be more imaginative in the details they describe. What changes from their

daily schedule do they envision? Would life be more or less hectic? Do any of them use any such technologies now (cell phone with Internet access, PDA, pager, etc.)? If so, how has it changed their lives? What might life be like if they were implanted with a computer chip?

3. This exercise requires students to have access to an Internet connection and to be able to view the videos on Stephens's Web site (see <www.picturingtexts.com>), and to write a short essay on whether they agree or not with his claim that videos provide new ways of thinking.

Since students are asked to back up their claims in this paper with evidence from these videos, it might be helpful to provide them with some strategies for doing so. Explain that the videos require the RealOne Player (downloadable for free from <www.real.com>—tell them to click on the link for the free player, not the $19.95 version). RealOne Player uses a timeline shown in hours, minutes, and seconds (for example, 01:30:04), which lets students refer to exact locations in the video as evidence for their argument. That way, you can find the exact segment a student cites. Also, referring back to the key term *description* in the beginning of the chapter, you might want to discuss how they can fully describe a scene they want to reference.

For other online examples of video journals, called video blogs or vlogs, visit the *Picturing Texts* Web site.

4. This exercise asks students to consider which images they would include with Stephens's essay. Review the key term *emphasis* in the front of the chapter and have students underline the main points in the essay. What images might help Stephens to communicate these main points more effectively? Also, are there any passages the students had difficulty understanding on the first read? Or a historical point that a visual would help? Ask students to find illustrations online (or draw some) that would benefit the text, searching <www.google.com> for words or themes that match what they want to illustrate.

SCOTT MCCLOUD, "Through the Door: Digital Production"

This excerpt from Scott McCloud's graphic book *Reinventing Comics* discusses the changes in work habits and work products for graphic artists since the use of personal computers became prominent in the late 1980s and early 1990s.

Focus.

1. This exercise asks students to look for specific evidence in McCloud's essay for what he claims is the computer's ability to allow children to explore first and understand later (see page 72 for an example that points to this claim). It requires them to read a visual and verbal text closely for evidence. Have them underline or circle specific evidence that might support McCloud's claim, and then ask them what percentage of their examples are only visual, or only verbal. Making a list on the chalkboard will help students to see where each of their examples falls.

   If students choose many verbal examples and few visual ones, ask them why. (Even if they agreed with Mitchell Stephens's argument in the first reading that visuals are important ways of communicating, they may not be used to analyzing visuals in a classroom setting and may choose more verbal examples because that is what they are used to instructors expecting from them. This may be a good time to revisit the expectations and goals of your course in relation to reading visual and verbal texts—and to reassure students that visual texts do matter, even in academic settings.)

2. This exercise asks students how McCloud's argument would change if he used only words. Although McCloud does in fact use lots of words to make his point, some of his images are instrumental to understanding his position. For instance, ask students to look at the single-column frame on page 70 that shows a graphic representation of McCloud

sitting on a technological totem pole. Ask them what it means to "interpret *new media* through the *filter* of the *old."* Then, ask them to describe what the totem pole means. Essentially, the totem pole represents the various kinds of media human culture has had: oral (represented by the bottom totem with three mouths—our oral culture, so to speak), written (which spawned the next totem), reading, radio, film, and television. Each media culture builds on the previous one.

Or, have students look at the frame in the middle of the top row on page 76 and ask them to interpret the graphic in that frame. Essentially, it mimics the written text in the same frame: the fact that some people have power and can afford computers and computer graphics programs also means that some populations cannot afford access, or have unreliable access to such technologies. But, McCloud also chose to create the graphic with the faces of three specific groups of people in the "no" sign. These groups could be interpreted to represent three groups less likely to have computers: African Americans, Latinos, and women. You could discuss how much more specific McCloud was able to be with drawings than he was with words.

Respond.

1. This exercise asks students to create their own visual texts by using the filters and effects in an image manipulation program such as Adobe Photoshop or Macromedia Fireworks. The image manipulation program Microsoft Image Composer is installed on computers with Microsoft Windows 1998 or later. Also, all Windows-based machines come with a free program called Paint. This program does not have filters and effects such as those mentioned in McCloud's essay, but students can draw, type, skew, rotate, and change colors of basic artwork. (You can find this program on most PCs by clicking Start/Programs/Accessories/Paint.) If you have access to such software, but students do not, make your own examples and bring them in. Or, if you have access to several laptops that you could bring in for the day, have students create their own examples in class in small groups.

Play with several of the filters and different looks for the digital art you or your students have created. After applying a filter, ask them what each of the new pieces reminds them of. (You can go back to the original artwork by clicking Edit/Undo on the toolbar of most programs.) Have them describe what effect each filter has on the original piece. Have them further explore the idea of filters by asking them to decide which filter would work best if they wanted a word or an image to look fuzzy, or like sand, or like a stained-glass window (or something else). In what situations might they need or wish to use such effects?

2. This exercise asks students to take a comic strip and to convey the same information using words alone. If students choose a frame from the McCloud piece, ask them to work in groups of two, each student using a different frame. Have each student write what he or she thinks his or her frame means, then pass the frame to another student. Then ask the other student to also write what he or she thinks that frame means. See if their interpretations match. If not, discuss why they think the two descriptions differed.

3. This exercise asks students to use clip art to explain a process or to tell a story without using words. Have them search online for "free clip art" (a search in quotation marks will produce good results). Or, search through the clip art that comes with Microsoft Word, Corel WordPerfect, or a similar word-processing program. To find the clip art in a program such as Microsoft Word, click on Insert/Picture/Clip Art (or a similar sequence). You will find the clip art gallery, which contains quite a few standard designs: for example, a person lecturing to a crowd, a stoplight, a guy holding a fist full of money, a stick figure scratching its head, a fancy car. Ask students to open Word, PowerPoint, or a similar program that uses clip art and to create a story by inserting the images into the document. If they need help deciding how specific pieces of clip art might make a story, review the key concepts of *narration*, *metaphor*, and *comparison and contrast* from the front of this chapter. If students do not have access to a computer to do this exercise, bring in old magazines and some blank paper and have them cut images out of the magazine and paste them up to create a narrative on paper.

Have students trade narratives and have each write a paragraph about what is happening in the clip-art story. Share these descriptions in class and discuss how close to the original idea the other student came. What limitations do students see when composing with visuals? They may conclude that visuals can represent many things, so a reader cannot always know for sure what a designer intends, unless that image is juxtaposed with words or other images.

M&Co, The Restaurant Florent Ad Campaign

This reading focuses on advertising for a restaurant in New York City; the advertising uses unconventional graphics.

Focus.

1. This exercise asks students to discuss why the designers at M&Co decided to use such unconventional advertising methods in promoting Restaurant Florent. Discuss with students the physical context of this restaurant—New York City, where new restaurants open and close with frequency. Ask why these advertisements could help the restaurant stay open. (Perhaps the unusual postcards and ads helped audiences to remember the restaurant and to think that eating there would be a unique dining experience.)

To take this exercise further, ask students to look at the postcard on page 80. In the interview that accompanies these advertisements, the owner, Florent Morellet, defines what he thinks this postcard means: a man and woman eating at a table (see paragraph 10). Ask students how Morellet figured out that the words represent a man and a woman. What characteristics of each gender are represented? (The woman has a napkin on her lap; she's wearing pumps and giggling. The man is wearing loafers and on the floor next to his shoes is his napkin.) How do words work as visuals in this text? It may help students to revisit the key concept of *metaphor* for this discussion. Some examples: the word "pumps" is placed on the page to be angled up from the floor, as real pumps would be; the word "napkin" is draped appropriately on the lap and floor; the food words are placed in the correct table positions.

Have students explore the intertextuality of the M&Co postcards. Bring in a copy of artwork by El Lissitsky such as *The Mischievous Boy*, available on the Getty Web site (see <www.picturingtexts.com>), or find some of the typographic works of F. T. Marinetti or Tristan Tzara. For more contemporary examples, see Keith Smith's *Text in a Book Format* or Johanna Drucker's work, one example of which is called *The History of the/my Wor(l)d* and is available from the Granary Books site (see <www.pictureingtexts.com>). Ask students to point out the similarities between their designs and the M&Co postcard. Each designer relies on typography as a strong visual component in the text, for one thing.

2. This exercise asks students to think about why the strategy of using Yellow Pages icons and stock photography was seemingly so successful. It asks students to explore *metaphor, unity,* and *comparison and contrast* by examining how the stock images are used. Using the postcard on page 82 as an example, bring in a copy of the Yellow Pages and ask students to find examples of ads that contain similar images. Compare the use of icons in the Yellow Pages and in the restaurant advertisement. Then, explore how some of the icons are oddly humorous, such as the image of the handgun. Ask students why they think the designer chose to juxtapose a gun with the words "New York." How do they think a New York audience would react to that juxtaposition of words and images? Another example is the cargo van image combined with the restaurant's address. Ask students to describe how each of the icons fits with the words that describe them and to discuss how the audience may see these symbols as hip and cool.

3. This question asks students to find narrative in the Restaurant Florent ads. Have students consider what each icon means to them. Then, ask if they can put all those meanings together to form a narrative.

Respond.

1. This assignment asks students to write an evidence-based response from Mitchell Stephens's point of view to Tibor Kalman, M&Co's designer for Restaurant Florent, who remarked that designers are wrong not to represent a product as it really is. How does Kalman represent things as they really are? (Notice how he points out where a man eating dinner has dribbled food all over his shirt and how that food is processed in the digestive system.) How far does he take these reality-based ads? Because students might assume that this question means that Stephens would disagree with Kalman, it might help to ask whether they think Stephens would agree with Kalman's methods—and why.

2. This assignment asks students to find other advertisements where the products represented are not necessarily shown in a positive light. They can go to <www.picturingtexts.com> for some places to find television commercials, including:

    • **AdCritic:** <www.adcritic.com/> This is a subscriber service, but they have several commercials available for free viewing if you sign in as a one-time guest.

    • **ClipLand:** <www.clipland.com/index.shtml> Only a few of the commercials listed on this site are available for viewing; this site works much like a music-sharing service wherein outside users allow others to stream video from a third-party location, which makes some of the links unreliable.

    • **Visit4info:** <www.visit4info.com/> This site has many ads from the United Kingdom for viewing.

    It may be easier for students to get a print-based ad from a magazine or videotape or to remember a commercial they have seen and to try to describe it in the response they write. Alternatively, you can tape a commercial and have the class all respond to the same one.

JESSICA HELFAND, "Squaring the Circle"

This short essay focuses on the importance of circles historically, from hieroglyphs and ideograms to electrical circuits, and as precursors to software interface designs as seen in wheel charts.

Focus.

1. This exercise asks students to think about why the circle is favored in many religious traditions, given the evidence Helfand offers in her essay. You may want to have students re-read the essay in class and to underline the portions of the text that offer examples of why the circle has been useful to so many groups of people. Ask them to determine what it is about the shape of the circle that allows diverse populations to find meaning in it.

2. This one asks students to decide whether they prefer digital clocks that show the exact time in hours, minutes, and seconds or analog clocks that show the time with moving hands. In this assignment, students may want to explore the differences Helfand cites regarding the rational and the rotational and what those terms mean to them. This assignment might best be approached by defining what Helfand means by these two terms (see paragraphs 6 and 7) and having students explain what personality characteristics they have that make them fit better into one category than the other.

Respond.

1. This exercise asks students to keep a log of all the circles they see. Suggest that they carry a camera with them or that they look for examples on the Web. Students may already know how to save images from the Web, but you can briefly explain it to them in this way:

> To save an image from a Web site, right-click with your mouse over the image. (On a Macintosh with a single-button mouse, hold the Control key while clicking to produce the

same effect.) A drop-down menu will appear. Click on the option for "Save Picture As" or "Download Picture to Disk" (or similar wording). Doing so will provide a pop-up box that will allow you to choose where to save the image on your computer or disk and what to call it.

Have students classify the circles they find according to subject matter. For a larger sample, ask students to bring their circles to class and classify them in small groups. What subjects are most likely to be represented by circles? You may also want to explore with students what other genres they can classify the circles into—informational, exploratory, analytical, and so on.

2. This exercise asks students to look at some museum Web sites (you can find several links to museums online on <www.picturingtexts.com>) or at works of art in a book and to find several examples that can be categorized as showing *centricity* (coming out of, or pulling toward, the center) or *eccentricity* (showing no true center but instead made up of grids), according to Arnheim's definition given on page 89. You may want to revisit the discussion on *unity*, where the use of grids was explored.

When students have chosen two or three examples, ask them to write a paragraph about how they illustrate centricity or eccentricity.

SMITHSONIAN MAGAZINE, "Covered in Glory"

This visual text shows twenty magazine covers from World War II, each displaying the American flag.

Focus.

1. This exercise asks students to classify the different themes represented by the cover of each magazine. Students may want to group the covers according to gender (there is a much larger proportion of women repre-

sented than men, begging the question of audience/readership during the war) or direction (does the flag point upward or downward? is there a connection between the kind of magazine and the way the flags are displayed in that grouping?). Do the classifications they discover affect meaning, or do all the covers have similar messages?

2. This one asks students to think about how these magazine covers focus on their usual subject matter while at the same time waving the flag. Some examples include *Silver Screen*, with an usher saluting the flag; *Wow Comics*, with a cartoon character flying with the flag; *Screenland*, which uses a proportionally larger image of a woman in a movie-star pose; and *House & Garden*, which positions a house in the background.

Respond.

1. This assignment asks students to account for commercial uses of the American flag, exploring the metaphors we associate with the flag and how we manipulate those metaphors for consumption. Ask students to find products or places that use the American flag as a sales tool and make a list of all the metaphors they can think of for the flag, such as patriotism and opportunity. Then have them make a list of products using the flag and the audiences for those products. Compare the two lists for common themes.

Another way for students to relate the idea of consumerism to patriotism is to examine the visual on page 92. What does this text say about products that use the American flag for monetary gain? Do students think it is appropriate for the flag to be used in this manner?

2. This assignment asks students to keep a list of all the flags and flag images they see in a day, describing why they think each flag is used in the context it is. You might ask them which ones surprised them the most, and why. Which, if any, seem most effective—and why? Least effective?

3. This assignment builds off the previous exercise. For this one, students should take their descriptions of the context and use of flag images and

write an essay discussing *why* the flags might be important to the people who display them in the given contexts. Also, they will need to relate why the flag is an important U.S. symbol. They may want to conduct informal interviews with friends and family to get their opinions about what the flag symbolizes.

4. This assignment asks students to revise the design of the flag and to write a paragraph explaining their changes. For an example of a redesigned flag, you may want to show students the Wisconsin State flag redesign (see <www.picturingtexts.com>), which explains three redesigns of the flag and why they were created. Ask students to list a few things about the United States that they would like to emphasize on their redesigned flag. What elements of being American are most important to them? What about living in the United States stands out the most when they think of what it means to be an American citizen?

Picture This

The purpose of this assignment is to get students to use a visual they have created—a snapshot of a place, in this case—and to describe it using words only (referring back to the key terms might help give them a structure to work from), visuals only (in some other form than a snapshot—clip art, perhaps), and then a combination of words and visuals. This assignment pulls together much of what students have learned in this chapter—combining their work with captions, description, and narrative to compose three new texts. Students will need time outside class to work on this larger assignment. Giving them a space to display their completed projects would also give them a chance to showcase their work and to describe orally what they intended to accomplish with the three texts they composed. Ask students to write about whether the words, the images, or the combination of both worked best to describe the place in their snapshot. Ask whether their opinion on which mode works "best" has changed since the beginning of the project.

2 looking closer

This chapter focuses on interpreting images, comparing two examples—Thomas Franklin's photo of firefighters raising the U.S. flag at the remains of the World Trade Center on September 11, 2001, and Joseph Rosenthal's photo of U.S. Marines raising the flag on Iwo Jima in 1945. With these two photos, the authors detail how to interpret an image by considering their immediate and broader contexts. On pages 114–15 is a list of questions designed to help students analyze images.

Following are some of the questions that need to be considered when analyzing any text, focused here on visual texts. We include examples from the two flag-raising photos, but you could also use images or other texts of your own choosing.

Immediate Context

Who is the author and how does his or her point of view affect the image? In this case, the authors were two war-correspondent photojournalists, taking photos for their respective news organizations. If individual authors cannot be determined, the point of view is usually evident in the publication medium in which the text appears.

What is the purpose? Although purpose can easily shift, the original intent of these photographs was to capture a news event. Yet when these images are reproduced elsewhere (such as on T-shirts or stamps), both the purpose and the context shift.

What are the medium and genre? Medium refers to the technology used to create and distribute a text, such as digital photography or print newspaper. In the case of these two photos, Rosenthal's was film while Franklin's was digital. But they are both in the genre of news photos. The genre helps us determine how to make meaning from a text; in a news photo, we assume the genre is intended to show a real news event, so we believe that the photo shows what actually happened. On the other hand, when we read a short story, we assume it is fictional.

What is the subject? The subject helps us to understand why a text is important and what its purpose is. For these two photos, they became easily recognized symbols of patriotism and emotional support in the face of tragedy.

Who is the audience? Although the intended audience for both these photos was newspaper readers who would presumably see them as representations of the events of the day, no author, photographer, or designer can know how his or her audience might interpret a text. For instance, once Franklin's photo was juxtaposed with Rosenthal's photo, the audience (and purpose) changed to those people who felt the events of September 11, 2001, were similar in importance to those of Rosenthal's photo and the events of 1945.

How is the text arranged? Arrangement refers to how the elements of a text are organized. Both Rosenthal's and Franklin's photos are arranged as triangles, with the flag at the highest point, which the photographers probably felt was the most important point in the shot.

Broader Context

What is the historical context? The Rosenthal photo was taken during World War II; the Franklin photo, on September 11, 2001. Even if we do not know the specific events (as may be the case with the Rosenthal photo for readers of this textbook), we have seen these photos enough to generalize what their historical contexts indicate—Americans in the midst of war. All texts can be read according to their historical context.

What are the cultural and social contexts? Even if readers have never been soldiers or known any soldiers, they understand the social and cultural impact of soldiers. No doubt, readers will have seen soldiers portrayed in movies or on television, and the meanings portrayed through those fictional soldiers (patriotism, nationhood, strength) can be applied to the soldiers in the photos. Of course, cultural and social connections made to some images may be humorous or serious or indifferent, depending on the context in which we understand those images. For instance (although this scenario is unlikely), if a person's only reference to soldiers is gathered from comic films such as *Private Benjamin*, then his or her interpretation of the two news photos will be drastically different from that of someone who has a family member in the Army.

What is the economic context? Although the economic conditions under which a text is created cannot always be known, our understanding of it changes if we know that it is being reproduced for economic gain. For the Franklin photo, the image began to appear almost immediately on T-shirts and other items for sale. These items may have been to support the Red Cross or other national relief efforts, but in this context of economic gain, the photos tend to be valued differently.

Snapshot

This assignment asks students to look at magazine ads with an eye for cultural, social, economic, and historical contexts. You could do this Snapshot in class, bringing in several magazines for students to look at or bringing in some ads torn out of magazines. Have students guess the contexts in which the ad was published based on the details of the compositional elements. For instance, students might notice that an ad pulled from a 1960s *Redbook* is in black and white, or has models wearing clothes that obviously do not resemble today's fashions. These contextual clues will help students date the ads. Next, ask students to take their own snapshots and write a short description of what clues in their own pictures will signal the context for future audiences.

Edward Hopper, *Nighthawks, 1942*
Mark Strand, "Hopper"
Joyce Carol Oates, "On Hopper's *Nighthawks, 1942*"

These three texts are grouped together with the first, Edward Hopper's painting *Nighthawks, 1942*, the inspiration for the other two—one an essay and the other a poem.

Focus.

1. This exercise asks students to look closely at Hopper's painting and to identify things that might lead us to see a story in it, as Strand and Oates do in their texts. If students have difficulty identifying individual elements, ask them what *they* see as the narrative the painting tells. Based on their stories, ask them to draw out what elements they focused on that helped them come up with that idea. Maybe they have been in a diner late at night and seen characters like those Hopper has painted? How do the four people in the scene interact? How does this shape what story is told? What's happening (or not happening) on the street? What time of the day or night do students think it is? What visual elements in the painting make them think so? Who are these people and why are they at the diner at this time of day?

2. This exercise asks students to look closely at the poetic text and to identify the story Oates tells, including the relationship between the people in the painting. Who are the two main characters in Oates's poem? Most of the poem focuses on the man and woman sitting together at the counter; few lines focus on the other two men. What does Oates believe the woman is thinking? Ask students to underline or read aloud a few passages attributed to the woman. Nearly the first third of the poem is written to help the audience understand the woman's story; then ten lines focus on the man, who is said to have left his wife and kids to be with the red-headed woman. Another long passage focuses on the woman's thoughts and finishes with her saying, "You

know I hate that: Stop!" You might point out how the poem goes back and forth between the woman and the man, with more time spent on the woman, and with only a few references to the other two men.

3. The third exercise asks students to study Strand's essay and to write about how their response to Hopper's painting is different from and similar to his—and why. Get students started by asking them to find descriptions in the essay that point to what Strand's life was like growing up in the 1940s. Then, ask them to make a list of what has changed about those things today. Do the storefronts and streets look the same? Did they view the world from the backseat of their parents' car? Have they ever been to Greenwich Village or to an all-night diner? (Or perhaps they can offer evidence that Strand is limited in his view that all-night diners and corners like the one in the painting are found only in the northeast United States.)

Respond.

1. This exercise asks students to gather outside research through interviews about people's responses to Hopper's painting and to incorporate their findings into a written response that includes their personal analysis of the painting. They may want to use some of the questions listed in Focus 3. You may also want students to note whether any of their respondents' replies differ from theirs and come to a conclusion about why. This assignment will help students understand how different audiences interpret visual texts. It may be helpful to note some useful interview techniques, including how to introduce the main idea of the assignment to those they interview and how *not* to ask both leading questions—starting with *why* and *how* always helps—and *yes-no* questions (which often start with "Do you think . . ."). Finally, remind students to prepare their questions and to write them down.

2. This assignment asks students to examine the compositional elements of a photo to determine its narrative. They may need help making connections between the compositional elements and subject matter of the photo and their own personal experience with similar subjects. For in-

stance, if they think the woman in curlers is getting her hair done to go somewhere fancy, they may not at first understand that their prior knowledge about dressing up to go out stemmed from having watched their parents do the same. That personal experience helped them to interpret the woman in the photo.

3. This assignment asks students to read a story that Ethan Canin wrote about incorrectly remembering details of a beloved picture and to write their own creative response to a photo they find or have. Canin's written response will help students see how personal information plays a large role in how we remember and interpret texts. Suggest that if they have an old family photo, they should use that. Or they could also find photos of people or events they do not know. If students cannot find a photo on their own, they could go to our Web site to see some representative photos. Or, they could have someone from home scan and email a photo or two.

JOEL STERNFELD, *McLean, Virginia, December 1978*

This photograph shows a person buying pumpkins from a produce stand on a pumpkin farm while a house fire rages in the distance.

Focus.

1. This exercise asks students to write a short description of the photo, noting what elements catch their attention first, and what details they focus on the most. In doing so, students can focus on what is emphasized in the photo and what details are important. Do they see the fire first? The farm stand? The field of rotting pumpkins? If they notice the stand first, why? Perhaps it is because it is the central element in the photo, a place that typically means emphasis. But then what do they see next? Why did the photographer frame the photo as he did? Also, it might help to point out smaller details—for instance, how the shape of the stand matches the shape of the burning house. What do

the similarities in shape signify to the students? How does it affect the subject matter and perhaps the purpose of the photo? Is it the farmer's house? If so, how does that change how we interpret the meaning of the photo?

2. This exercise asks students to reinterpret the meaning of the photo if the person buying pumpkins were instead positioned next to the stand watching the firefighters. How do the subject of the photo and its purpose change based on where the person is standing? Would the person seem more invested if he were paying more attention? If the students do not notice that the person buying pumpkins is a firefighter—he's wearing the same yellow firejacket, black firehat, and black boots we normally see on a firefighter—point out this detail and ask them if it changes the impact of the photo yet again. Have them speculate why the firefighter is buying pumpkins when his co-workers are trying to quench the flames on the ladder truck. Ask them where their eyes are drawn to in the photo now. What other details can they point out—and what do they mean?

3. This assignment asks students to compare a traditional landscape photo in which nature is represented as beautiful, with Sternfeld's photo, which contradicts that idea. You may want to bring in some photos of a landscape, asking students to list all the compositional elements they find in the traditional landscape. After they have this list, ask them to compare that to Sternfeld's photo to see if any of the points match, writing down those that match in a second column. Afterwards, ask them to list in a third column all of the elements in Sternfeld's photo that are unique to his text. Are there any items in the third column that could be considered beautiful, even though they may not traditionally be considered so—the orange flames of the fire, for instance?

Respond.

1. This exercise asks students to determine how cropping affects emphasis and even subject matter, showing them how to create a viewfinder and having them position it over different areas of the photo. For in-

stance, they may choose to show only the fireman buying a pumpkin. This creates much different subject matter than showing the flaming house as well. Prompt students to discuss how the subject shifts according to the way they crop the photo. Are some croppings better suited to certain audiences than others?

2. This exercise challenges students to create an unconventional greeting card using Sternfeld's photograph. It might help students to see some examples of funny or surprising greeting cards; bring some in or send them to online greeting card sites such as those for Blue Mountain or Hallmark (see <www.picturingtexts.com>) to explore the greeting card genre. Students should consider what occasion the card is for— Thanksgiving (gone wrong)? Halloween? a birthday (maybe there were too many candles on the cake)? a get-well card (things couldn't get much worse!)? You could bring in colored pens and paper for students to create the cards in class.

JOHN SZARKOWSKI, "ON APPLES GROWN BY IRRIGATION"

This postcard of apples and its accompanying description hint at a relationship between a certain Miss Annie and Jim A. in 1907.

Focus.

1. The first exercise asks students to explore postcards showing their school. This is a good opportunity to get them to read the cards with an eye for audience, purpose, and subject. If you have postcards from the school or area, bring them to class and do this exercise in class, in small groups. Have each group analyze one of the postcards to determine why elements are used to serve a particular purpose for the audience. Ask students if they think these are the best images to use to represent the school. If they think there are others that are better, discuss what those are and why the designer chose those he or she did. For instance, some school postcards feature local shops or bookstores; do students

think they should feature places students frequent more (such as a local tavern or fast-food place)? You could also discuss audience—who would buy these postcards and who would receive them?

2. This assignment asks students to focus on how trivial subjects become less trivial when they are photographed. Bring in some postcards (or look at the ones in the previous exercise) and ask students to notice what ordinary or odd details they see and why they think the designer would include them on the postcard. For people who have never visited the area, what do these details show? Why? Are there stories behind the details?

3. This exercise asks students to look at the composition of the postcard to determine why Szarkowski sees the image as "moving, memorializing." Students may want to focus on unity, balance, proportion, and pattern. How do these four elements work in this postcard? You may also need to define pomologist (a person who studies fruit).

Respond.

1. This assignment will help students explore how context shifts meaning and to see that a photo of apples such as this one can be used to convey various different messages. Ask students what they associate with apples—sayings, metaphors, themes, any associations they have with apples. These might include "An apple a day keeps the doctor away," apple pie, worms, or Adam and Eve. Then list all the ways an image of apples can be used: for example, on a calendar to represent harvesting season, as a gift to a teacher, as the forbidden fruit. Have students jot notes on the meanings of each of these associations and then write an analysis of how changes in context offer new interpretations of a simple object.

2. This assignment asks students to write an analysis of why the compositional elements of the photo cause Szarkowski to read it as artwork rather than as a snapshot. Refer them to the vocabulary in Chapter 1 and discuss how some terms can be applied to read the text. Focus on the balance, pattern, and unity of the apples in relation to the open

frame of the image (created by the apples sitting in front of an object the audience cannot entirely see). Students can use this in-class discussion, as well as other terms such as description and comparison of colors, in their written analysis.

3. This exercise asks students to create several examples of still-life compositions using apples and to write about which compositions are more artistic than others. Refer them to the still-life images given in the textbook on page 133 to discuss how point of view (in the angle the photos are taken), comparison (in the subject matter of the ketchup bottle and crooked fork versus more traditional still-life compositions), and pattern (in the lines of the tabletop, or number of bowls) all help to create artistic works.

Bruce Grierson, "Shock's Next Wave"

This article discusses how the advertising industry sometimes shocks us into paying attention to certain products.

Focus.

1. This exercise asks students to consider if the heavyhanded tactics that ads used in the 1950s and 1960s are still used today. Ask them to name ads—print, television, or Web—where they see forms of "mind control" at work. Bring in an ad of this kind if you can—perhaps one like the "advertrocities" mentioned in the last part of the article—and discuss it in class. Ask students if they are shocked by the ad; if not, have they seen it before, or does it just not shock them? Why? For those students it does shock, how does it do so? For that matter, does Grierson's article shock students? Some of the language—the word "fuck," for example—can be shocking—especially to see or hear it in an academic environment. How do they react to its use? Have them question why they think he uses such language and if it serves a purpose?

It is productive to discuss with students how language choice impacts the purpose of a text when they start writing papers in which they have freedom to shape their own topics and draw deeply on their own opinions. Given such open-ended assignments, students will invariably ask if they can use colloquial or offensive language. One response to this might be to ask them if they need to use such words and what purpose they serve. Sometimes, as in Grierson's essay, such language does serve a purpose; most often in student essays it does not.

2. This exercise asks students to find ads that correspond to each of the three levels of shock ads Grierson presents—visceral, intellectual, and soul. It may be hard to find examples of each of these, but one place to check would be online at AdBusters (see <www.picturingtexts.com>). Or, if possible, assign students to videotape a certain channel to see if they find any cable channels that are probably more likely to contain such shock ads. Students may collectively remember some such ads and you can discuss how these ads fit into the classifications Grierson provides.

Alternatively, if finding good examples of the three kinds of ads is difficult, you could discuss in class (after looking for examples) why students had a harder time finding some kinds. Was anyone able to find a soul-shocking ad? What did they do to find it? (This could also lead into a discussion of thorough research habits.) If no one found shocking ads, discuss why there seems to be a lack of them. Is it where they searched? The media?

3. This exercise asks students to think about audiences for shock ads. You could start by thinking about where such ads are found, and then consider the audiences to which those publications or channels cater. They are probably not likely to find shock ads on the Women's Entertainment (WE) network or on Lifetime, while they may find them on MTV (embedded, even, in some of the shock reality series on television now). Ask students who the audiences are for these channels and why these audiences would or would not prefer shock ads.

Respond.

1. This assignment asks students to find and analyze shock ads. Point students to places to find ads, if they have difficulty finding them on their own. Some online resources are located at <www.picturingtexts.com>. One way to approach this assignment is to have students look at Benetton ads and discuss how they've changed over time.

2. This assignment asks students to analyze how one shock ad plays off the audience's values. Again, point students to <www.picturing texts.com> for online resources. Also, some cable channels, including HBO and MTV, run shows or commercials that might be shocking to students. HBO also runs a show called "Shock TV" on which students might be able to find examples. You can perhaps bring in a sample videotape to discuss in class.

3. This assignment asks students to reflect on whether they are shocked by anything these days. One way to approach this assignment would be to ask students whether they were shocked by any of the language or metaphors Grierson uses in his article. Or, ask if they remember a time when they were shocked to hear or see something—when their values were questioned by words or images—but then became accustomed (or not) to that language or image. You might try to videotape and show students the opening credits for CBS's show *CSI*. There is a quick montage of images, one of which is a person hitting a dummy over the head to crack its skull. (In 2003, this show aired in primetime, and also aired in reruns on the cable channel TNN. The original show, *CSI*, and *not* its spinoff *CSI: Miami*, has a shocking image in the opening credits.) You may want to warn students in advance that there is graphic violence (what does that mean to them?) in the clip. After viewing the opening, ask if any images startled or shocked them. Ask if there is a difference between being *startled* and being *shocked*. Which does this image do to them? How would they explain the difference between the two words? Does *startling* someone affect their values to the same extent that *shocking* someone might?

Additionally, you could discuss with students the television and film rating system. The history of the ratings system and details on how it works can be found on the Motion Picture Association of America's Web site (see <www.picturingtexts.com>).

Picture This

This assignment asks students to create a postcard for the town in which they live and to write an essay explaining what their postcard represents about the place. It might help students to understand the humor of the Michigan Technological University postcard to bring a map of North America to class and to show them where Houghton, Michigan, is located (connected to Wisconsin, it is situated on a tiny peninsula in the middle of Lake Superior). Ask students how they might visually represent a local joke or event for an audience that does not know the area. Ask them to narrow their audience—not just to all visitors to the area or their family. Ask them to think about what kinds of people would like to get a postcard such as the one they create. Ask them to include the description of their audience and the purpose of the postcard in their written explanation.

Context and Questions for the Gallery of Images

1. *The Human Condition.* Painting by René Magritte, 1933.

   René Magritte was a surrealist painter from Belgium. His work meticulously renders both physical and psychological states of being, often employing visual puns that question our assumptions about what we see and what we think we see. This painting is concerned with illusion: what we see, what we see when we look closer, how we try to capture these perceptions. What do you think this had to do with the human condition? What does the window signify?

2. *World Trade Center Mural.* Austin, Texas, 2001.

   This mural appeared on the side of an Austin laundromat after September 11, 2001. It incorporates the events of that day with angels and the Virgin of Guadeloupe, to whom many miracles have been attributed. Her shrine in Mexico City has been visited by millions of Catholics, especially those of Hispanic descent, and she is a beloved part of that culture. How does the composition affect what is emphasized in this reinterpretation of that day? Why did the artist choose to render both towers as standing? How does the artist bridge the earthly and the spiritual worlds, and New York and Austin?

3. *Chicago 1959/61*. Photo by Yashuhiro Ishimoto. Ishimoto lives in both Japan and the United States, and his work reflects both sensibilities. In this photo, the young man's hand looks to be holding a mask. Looking closer, however, we see that this is an illusion. The dark and white no-tan pattern confuses foreground and background to further emphasize this illusion. In what other ways does Ishimoto balance opposites, and to what effect?

4. *Untitled* (Jasper County, Iowa). Photo by John Vachon, 1940. This documentary photograph has a closed form that focuses our attention on the women's faces—that makes us look closer. The strong triangular shape visually groups the figures and unifies the image. Light is also used as a unifying element. How does the use of light enhance the emotional experience of this image? How does the light differ from the light used in Hopper's *Nighthawk* painting?

5. *Trailer Light*. Photo by Warren Wheeler. By capturing the shadows on the side of the trailer, the photographer allows us to see a part of the life of those who lived inside. Can the shadow of the rockinghorse be interpreted as a visual metaphor? If so, for what?

6. *Untitled #5*. Photo by Anna Gaskell, 1996. Gaskell's photos use posed figures, artificial lighting, unusual camera angles, and close-up cropping to suggest ambiguity between reality and fiction, what we see and what we imagine. This photo is from her *Wonder* series, in which she explores issues of girlhood through allusions to *Alice in Wonderland*. How does her use of scale, point of view, cropping, and lighting contribute to this photograph's message?

3 making lives visible

This chapter covers several genres with which students are likely to be familiar: scrapbooks, memory books, memoirs, autobiographies, and diaries. In examining the history of these genres, the authors point to the visual aspects: the people who kept such books often included visual texts. For instance, several historical diaries show how a diary entry might be illustrated with drawings. This style of incorporating visuals with words carries through to more contemporary and technologically sophisticated texts, such as Joseph Squier's *Urban Diary*, an online visual representation of a day in the life of the designer. This chapter also points out that much is left out of such personal narratives—writers always *choose* which details to show (and not), which way to point the camera, what to leave in, and what to crop out.

Snapshot

In this exercise on page 168, students are asked to determine how photo opportunities—the photo provided here being one example—of social events are composed by the photographer and subjects. In the case of the photo here, the father is posing the daughter. How do the photos that students encounter, such as their yearbook photos or sports team photos, represent deliberate composition by the photographer? How do people stand in such photos? What are they wearing? How can readers determine what the event of the photo might be by the visual clues in the photos? What happens when an element in the photo is askew, such as when one person in a group photo blinks or turns his or her head?

NANCY CARPENTER, "And My Hats Were Prettier"

This reading includes a photo and a personal narrative by Nancy Carpenter, an African American woman from North Carolina, about an important incident in her life, shopping for hats in a store that had formerly been "Whites Only."

Focus.

1. This exercise explores the notions of metaphor, audience, and context by asking students to interpret the importance of the book's name, *Crowns*. What significance do crowns hold? Who gets to wear crowns and why? The subtitle of the book, *Portraits of Black Women in Church Hats*, suggests an occasion when the women wear hats. Ask students how this connects to the book's title. What about church relates to crowns?

2. This exercise asks students to compare the photo with Carpenter's written text. Is the tone of the written text similar to that of the photo? Do the two texts contrast? (Perhaps students would not have expected Carpenter to be smiling so confidently in the photo.) How does the décor add to our understanding of her? Ask students to discuss how the photo was composed for publication in the book about hats. Do they think Carpenter always dresses in pearls and a suit? (Perhaps—but it may prompt a discussion about how people portray themselves.)

Respond.

1. This question asks students to think about styles and trends and to consider why they dress as they do and what their own style "says" about them. Ask them to trace their clothing to a particular fashion trend—where they first saw it and why they chose to adopt it, or remind students about the different styles that have been popular over the last century—for example, how women could not show their ankles at the turn of the twentieth century, how women were expected to

wear dresses and men suits and hats in the early decades of the twentieth century, or how students in many schools are not allowed to wear shorts to class. Bring in a book or show an Internet site that details fashion history for the last several decades and ask students to describe how each trend represented a certain idea about that decade. One good resource site is located at Costumes.org; check out the twentieth-century links at the bottom of the Web page (*see* <www.picturingtexts.com>).

2. This assignment asks students to interview a friend or someone who wears some trendy item and to write about the significance of that trend and what it says about those who embrace it. They may need help extrapolating from one interview to a broader consideration of a fashion trend and how it reflects larger cultural ideas and ideals. If students do not have access to a camera to photograph this assignment, make sure they fully describe the subject of their essay.

3. This assignment asks students to think beyond their immediate peer group, exploring the same question as the preceding one, but with someone of their parents' generation instead. They might ask about memorable changes in their clothing styles—and what prompted those changes.

4. This assignment asks students to explore personal memories represented by a piece of clothing. If they need help, ask them to recall, for example, what they were wearing when they first arrived at college, had their first school picture taken, went on their first date, or were confirmed. Then, have them write about what they wore and why they still remember what they wore.

SABRINA WARD HARRISON, "I Talked to Nana This Morning"

A journal page recalling a grandmother's advice, this text includes both handwritten text and photos.

Focus.

1. This exercise asks students to focus on the composition of the verbal and visual elements in this text. If they read the words first, how does the image affect what they have read, and vice versa? Ask students about the significance of the slanted lines and the upside-down photo of a woman's torso (the artist's?) at the top of the page. Why is the woman in the photo looking outside the frame rather than directly at the camera? One answer might be that if she looked directly at the camera, her gaze would be emotionally stronger, which would perhaps suggest a different purpose. The same could be said of the partial torso. Perhaps by including only the torso, the designer was pushing the audience to focus on the area where the heart is, in relation to the lines about "falling in love." You may also want students to think about the colors Harrison uses: Why the dark and somber quote at the top and the bright, sunny colors below?

2. This exercise asks students to focus on Harrison's use of capitalization. It seems she wanted to have the audience (and perhaps herself) focus on certain key terms, which she capitalized: KNOW IN time, I SHOULD tAKE CARE of the PAIN, DON't PICK At IT, FALLING IN LOVE. You may want to write the capitalized words on an overhead or the chalkboard—and then ask students to analyze why Harrison chose to emphasize them. Do they merely highlight certain phrases, or do they more likely summarize key ideas?

Respond.

1. This exercise asks students to complete a written description of someone who has been influential in their lives. Consider having students do this assignment in class, with a few minutes at the beginning of class to brainstorm. If they have difficulty choosing someone, ask them to make a list of several important moments in their lives and then to write down next to that list the people who were influential in helping them through those moments.

2. For this assignment, students create a scrapbook about a person who is important to them. It may be a friend or relative (such as the person they wrote about in the previous assignment) or hero. Keep in mind that their scrapbooks can be on paper or they could be digital—Web pages or Photoshop collages, perhaps. Ask them to think about the person's key traits and have them collect images or objects that would match.

3. This assignment asks students to translate their scrapbook into words alone. They should touch upon why they chose this person and these images. If they included poems or other texts, they should explain *how* those texts are important for writing about the person.

BELL HOOKS, "In Our Glory: Photography and Black Life"

This reading explores black culture and photography—the lack of the black family as a subject of photos in museums and the misrepresentations (or under-representations) of black people in artwork and, thus, in history. hooks focuses on a photo of her father taken before she was born to discuss how family members, as well as individuals in society, read images differently. Students can read this selection as one that moves from the personal (of hooks's family photo) to the more universal (of how the history of African Americans in the United States has affected how America sees black culture).

Focus.

1. This is a good exercise for exploring how the context of a personal photo or image affects what we see and what we do not. Why does hooks want the photo of her father? Why was she so disappointed to lose her favorite childhood photo? Are these two events related? How would students react if their favorite photo were misplaced?

2. Ask students if they remember a time when any of their siblings or relatives remembered an event differently or reacted to a photo differently than they did. Can they explain why this happened? What about

that photo can they remember, even without having it with them? Are their favorite photos of happy memories? If any student remembers a photo from an unhappy time (and he or she is willing to share that event with the class), ask him or her to explain why he or she remembers it. If it is possible for students to bring these photos to class, pass them around and ask others to say what they think is happening in each photo. How many times can they guess correctly from the visual clues? Why do they think that is?

3. This exercise asks students to contextualize their own family photographs, to remember how they are displayed, and what thematic elements, if any, link the photos on each wall or page. This assignment may pose challenges if students do not remember how the photos are grouped or if the family does not display or keep photos. An alternative way to do this assignment would be for you to bring in a collection of photos (framed or in an album) and to ask students to classify the photos according to genre—party photos, family reunion photos, photos of older relatives, vacation photos, and so on. Additionally, you could ask students to classify the photos according to time periods.

Respond.

1. This assignment asks students to write an essay about a favorite photo. Asking them to imagine an audience a hundred years from now might help them to explain what elements in the photo make it their favorite. Remind students they will need to describe thoroughly with words what is happening in the photo.

2. This assignment asks students to analyze a grouping of photos on their campus, such as photos of faculty members, student sports teams, or archived images in the library. Remind them to use the key terms covered in Chapter 1 in their analysis.

3. This assignment asks students to create a visual narrative of snapshots to give to a friend as a gift and to write a letter explaining why they have chosen these photos. It will call upon them to make choices and to think about how the photos they gather tell a story. Ask students to

think about how their audience will read their visual narratives—do the frame sizes or positions matter in terms of which frame will be read first or last? If students do not have their own photos, you can provide some sample photos for them, or they can cut photos out of magazines.

BILLY COLLINS, "Litany"

This poem shows students how a written text can be visually stimulating through the use of metaphors. Some students may wonder why "Litany" doesn't rhyme and will find it difficult to discover the natural rhythm of the language that Collins uses. It may be useful to read the poem aloud so that students can hear the nuances of the speaker. It would also be useful to discuss the metaphors in the poem.

Focus.

1. This exercise asks students to determine how the epigraph affects their reading of the poem. Epigraphs act as context for poems (or other texts), helping the audience to start reading with a particular image or idea in mind. After reading the epigraph at the beginning of Collins's poem, students might expect a traditional love poem instead of one with ironic twists. You may want to ask students what they think the poem is about since it never uses the word "love." How do they know what the poem means?

2. Answers will vary greatly for this one, so it might be a good question to use first. If anyone suggests that part of the poem is funny, or sad, or surprising, ask them why they think Collins wanted to include such humor in the poem. Why not write a typical love poem? Do they like the poem? Are they likely to remember it? Why?

3. This question gets students to examine the language of the poem. You may want to read a typical love poem for comparison (you'll find links to some on <www.picturingtexts.com>). Or, have students underline the passages they find startling in Collins's poem. The most obvious places are at the beginning of stanza 2, in stanza 5 (when the speaker

switches to describing himself), and in the last stanza (when the speaker reminds the person being addressed that he or she is still the "bread and the knife").

This discussion might lead into an examination of the role of the poet within a poem—typically students will assume that the poet is the speaker of the poem. In this case, that would mean that Collins is the speaker of the poem, and that he is speaking to his lover. Ask students to put themselves into the role of the speaker. Who would they likely say these things to? Is it necessarily a woman that the speaker is talking about? A man? An adult or a child? The language in the poem does not indicate any gender or age. What does this say about who is speaking in the poem? And what is Collins's role as poet—is he also the speaker? It is possible, but by considering several different scenarios in which this poem might be read (a parent to an irrepressible child, perhaps?), students may begin to imagine the separation between poet and speaker, which signals the creative genre—the fiction—of poetry.

Respond.

1. This assignment asks students to write two stanzas in which they incorporate what images they might be, as Collins has done. Start by asking them to point out where in the poem the metaphors offer strong visual clues (these occur on nearly every line of the poem). Another helpful hint would be to ask them what their favorite things to do are and suggest they use those as metaphors. For instance, if they like watching NASCAR races, they might write the line: "I am the taste of Jeff Gordon's victory milk." Tell them to be as specific and detailed as possible and to use their five senses to help them think about how something might look, feel, sound, and so on.

2. This assignment asks students to add images to Collins's poem and should lead them to think about whether the images help or hinder the meaning of the poem for them. You may want to have students illustrate a stanza or two by drawing the nouns Collins uses. For instance,

to illustrate the marsh birds suddenly in flight, they might include a visual of several egrets or seagulls taking off from a swampy area.

You could also have students illustrate the poem by asking them to draw or use clip-art images that *do not* exactly mimic the language of the poem. This will be much harder, but ask them to think about what the metaphors in the poem *look* like. Then ask them to think about what those images they see mean in words.

3. This assignment asks students to create a visual version of Collins's poem. If possible, have students scan in their artwork and create a sequenced poem on a computer, in a program such as iMovie, Photoshop, or PowerPoint. Go to <www.picturingtexts.com> for some examples of a visuals-only poem produced by students. If computer access is not available, have students draw their poems on transparencies (give each student several sheets—one for each stanza would work well). Having them work in groups for this assignment might be a good idea. When they are done, have one student in the group read the poem aloud while another student shows the corresponding visual version on an overhead projector.

BARBARA KRUGER, "Memory Is Your Image of Perfection"

Kruger's work comments on the image of women in the United States, using an X-ray that shows a woman wearing high heels and jewelry. She adds words to the visuals to make her argument more explicit.

Focus.

1. This exercise prompts students to discuss the piece's purpose in relation to its cultural and social implications. How do the woman's accessories relate to the written text?

2. This question asks students to determine the audience of Kruger's text. How does the use of the second-person address ("your") imply to whom Kruger is speaking? She seems to be placing the ability to comment or change the argument she presents on individual audience members. What if she had used the first-person "our" instead? Does the tone feel more or less accusatory with the change of pronouns? Ask students to narrow the audience—to whom does the "you" refer? Who is likely to identify with the woman in the X-ray? All women? Certain women? All men? Ask students to refer to textual clues that support their interpretations. More than one audience grouping is likely, so ask them to explain why they have chosen their particular group. Do all of the elements in the text corroborate their theory?

3. This question asks students to examine the purpose of using certain typefaces and how typefaces impact the meaning of the text. If you have access to a computer with different typefaces on it, type one word several times onscreen and then change the typeface for each instance of that word. Make one script-like, using a font such as Edwardian Script or Lucida Handwriting; one traditional, using a serif font such as Times New Roman or Helvetica; one modern, using a sans-serif font such as Arial Black or Eurostile; and one decorative, using a font such as Jokerman or Curlz. If you do not have a computer in class, you can make a transparency with these typefaces on it. Ask students to determine situations in which they might see these fonts—for example, a Yellow Pages ad for a moving company, a flashy magazine ad for a computer company, a party invitation, a bridal shower invitation, or a flyer for a new rock band. Ask them to describe how each typeface might work in different situations based on their visual impact. Why might a decorative font such as Curlz be used more effectively in a party invitation than for a rock band flyer or a bridal shower invitation? Is Curlz "strong" enough to promote a band? Is it formal enough for a bridal shower?

Respond.

1. This assignment asks students to compose a short commentary on an advertisement, taking into consideration how visual and verbal ele-

ments work together to make the purpose of the ad fit its audience. Have students look at each of the ads and discuss the typefaces, their sizes, and how these choices impact what the ad is communicating. Also, ask students to identify the subjects of the ad. For instance, in the Planned Parenthood postcard, there are four women of varying ethnicities—why is this important? Why does the Choose Life ad use only written text? Why is it important to the message? (The difference could be discussed in context of who has more rights—women or children.)

This assignment may cause much discussion in your class. While you may embrace such discussion, it is also possible to ask students to use their opinions on the matter to help determine why these ads are effective for their respective audiences. You may have to remind students that if they disagree with one side's opinion, it may not be accurate to say that their ads are not effective—remind them that, after all, they are not the target audience for that ad.

2. This assignment asks students to compare the visual by Cynthia and Richard Selfe to Barbara Kruger's and Lorna Simpson's work and then to create a similar text. After students have analyzed the three examples in the textbook, ask them to think about what they would like to express to an audience. Do they have a cause they would like to promote or an idea they feel needs more coverage in the media? Ask them what everyday problems they encounter. For instance, do they feel the draft age needs to be raised? The driver's license test age lowered? Do they believe all students should go through religious training? Do they want to work on changing the dress code policies at their school? Do they want to send a message to their parents that the students are responsible? Ask students what visuals come to mind when they think about their topic. What key words do they want to emphasize in their texts? How might those key words and visuals correspond and be sequenced? Make sure students write an artist's statement describing what their work means and how the words and visuals work together to create that meaning.

You may have students draw what they need, find images on the Web and copy them into Word to add the written text to them, or take digital pictures in class and use Photoshop or another image-manipulation program to add the written text. They could even animate each image in ImageReady or PowerPoint if they want to create a moving sequence.

3. This assignment asks students to condense their combination of words and images to fit on one postcard. What topic do they want to emphasize? Students may want to work with the same topic they used for the second exercise, creating a new text that synthesizes all the ideas they come up with for that assignment. Or, they can start from scratch and create a new postcard containing words and images that support an idea or organization. Make sure students choose a topic or organization with which they are already familiar, unless you want them to research a new area. They will need to decide who their audience for the postcard is. You may have students write a short letter explaining why they have created this postcard and send it to the represented organization.

Michelle Citron, "What's Wrong with This Picture?"

This reading explores how we remember and interpret personal images, such as home movies, according to what we want to remember about events. It also explores what is left out of such personal images. Citron's essay is in two parts, on facing pages. One page describes why and how she reacted to viewing her family home movies with such vehemence. The facing page, which runs parallel to the first and has a different typeface, comments on the tradition of moviemaking and how it became a somewhat exploitative medium, producing much family embarrassment. This second section includes a running strip of still frames from Citron's own home movies, to which she refers throughout.

Focus.

1. This exercise asks students to think about how they read texts that combine verbal and visual elements in a genre in which they may be used to reading only words (such as an essay). Based on their knowledge of how images enhance or offer more meaning to a text, how did

they read the movie frames Citron provided? If they looked at the frames first and then read the words, were they surprised by the difference between the two? While the movie frames appear to be of a happy family, Citron's verbal text negates that idea and offers alternative interpretations to the visuals.

2. You may want to do this assignment before students read Citron's text. It asks students to read only the images or only the words and to determine if the meaning changes. It may be useful to do this exercise in class, before assigning the reading, by showing a transparency copy of a page or two (paragraphs 4–6 of the left-hand pages would work well, accompanied by the first right-hand page containing the initial frames of "The Promenade").

First show students the movie frames only and ask them to narrate what they think is happening. Next, show the whole right-hand page, with movie frames and the sans-serif text. Ask them why they think the home movie frames might add meaning to the historical essay they accompany. Does this juxtaposition make sense to the students? Do the visuals communicate the same message as the written words? If not, why would the author place the contrasting visual and verbal texts on the same page?

Next, show students the left-hand page with the verbal text only and ask them to read those paragraphs. How does what is written correspond to what they have already read? to what they have seen in the movie frames? How does the personal narrative change their reading of the visuals? What does the memoir say about what the family was really like that we cannot see from the movie?

3. This exercise asks students to examine the idea of an ideal family within the context of Citron's text. What personal experiences do the students have that help them form their ideas of an ideal family situation? Does any of them have an "ideal" family? Do some students feel they have a less-than-ideal family? What makes them think there is such a thing as an ideal family? Are social or economic factors involved? In what contexts can an ideal family be found, if it is even possible?

Respond.

1. This assignment asks students to write a narrative about what a collection of their personal photos tells—and to consider what is left out of that narrative. What elements did they purposefully omit to make the story more ideal? For instance, if their photo collection is about a camping trip they took with a best friend, did they also include the details about when they got into a fight over who would use the flashlight? Did the practical joke involving the raccoon make it into the narrative? How about the context of the trip—to get away from divorcing parents?

2. This assignment invites students to examine the broader contexts in which families are represented in advertisements. Students should write an essay based on their analysis of the narratives these images present. You may want to have students start this assignment in class by asking them to make a list of what each visual representation says about family. Ask them who the audiences are for the magazines where their ads appeared—how do the visuals appeal to the audience?

3. This assignment asks students to create a storyboard for a home movie. The textbook gives several examples of Web sites that offer help and/or templates on storyboarding, and <www.picturingtexts.com> has even more. Here are a few things to remind students about when they start their storyboards: a. They don't have to be well-drawn, just understandable. b. They should include as many sequences as possible. If students want to film a scene where they drive from home to school and it's raining, for instance, they should draw several storyboards, including one of them putting rain gear on, one driving the car with the rain hitting the windshield (and maybe where we can see the wipers going), one arriving at school and walking through the rain to the building, and finally, one storyboard in which they arrive at the location (such as a classroom) where they wanted to go. Students might otherwise skip these steps and draw themselves only leaving the house and sitting in the classroom, but the action is contained in those intermediate scenes. As with their writing, their drawings should be as descriptive as possible. Storyboards are similar

to a flipbook, wherein the major actions need to be shown. c. Last, if they want to show a timed sequence (maybe a fast action scene?), they should indicate how long the scene will take at the top of the storyboard. Most templates they find online will provide a place for such time indicators.

GREG HALPERN AND FRANK MORLEY, "The Man Didn't Even Know I Was There"

This reading combines a first-person narrative from Morley, a janitorial worker at Harvard, with photos taken by Halpern, a student at Harvard during the living wage campaign.

Focus.

1. This exercise asks students to discuss the compositional elements that make the Harvard workers so visible in Halpern's photos. You may need to point out that the workers are the central element in each frame and are much larger than any of the background elements. Some of the photos resemble formal portraits, in contrast perhaps to the low-paying positions Morley describes.

2. This exercise asks students to think about how written narratives can be especially persuasive in certain contexts, including Harvard's living wage campaign. Start this discussion by asking students to look only at the photographs of the workers. What descriptions can they come up with based on the contextual clues of each photo? Then, ask them to study Frank Morley's narrative. Do they know people who live similarly hectic lives? How much information does the narrative *add* to the photos? Ask students if knowing about these workers' lifestyles changes the way in which they engage with the photos.

Respond.

1. In this assignment, students will write about their own experiences seeing custodians at their school. Start this assignment by asking stu-

dents if they know the names of the people on the custodial staff in their dorms or buildings. (Even students who feel they are in touch with such workers at their school may be surprised by this question.) Did this reading change the way they think about those workers? If so, why? How would the students feel if they made minimum wage and had to pick up other students' trash all day? Some students may work on campus and perform similar jobs, but have them expand their notions of a student job to someone who does a similar job for a living, without the benefit of parental help or student loans. Try to get them to imagine what it might be like to work such a job and support a family. Although the textbook suggests that students include images in their written texts, you may want to brief them on the delicacies of taking a photograph of someone they don't know.

2. This excercise asks students to think about how narratives can be more persuasive than visuals. Start discussion by asking students to look at only the pictures of the workers presented in the book. What arguments do these images make about the Harvard Living Wage Campaign? Then, ask them to read Frank Morley's narrative. Does it argue for their attention more—or less—effectively than the images do? You might ask in particular about the hectic lifestyle Morley describes— does this description make him sound like someone closer to home? How much information does the narrative add to the photos? What about the reverse? What conclusions can students draw about the effectiveness of visual and verbal texts for a campaign of this kind?

SHARON HAREL, JUDITH WILDE, AND RICHARD WILDE, "Typographic Portraits"

This reading shows how even business cards make lives "visible."

Focus.

1. This exercise asks students to choose which card is effective in certain contexts and how each card displays the personalities of the designer.

Their overall favorites may have more to do with students' own personalities than composition. Ask students to explain why they chose certain cards over others, or vote in class to see which card is the class's favorite. Then discuss its compositional elements to decide what message it communicates.

2. This question asks students to focus on what audiences can know about designers based on the typographic elements they choose. For this exercise, ask students to look closely at several of the cards and to decide what effect a certain typeface creates. Having students describe the typographic elements will help them determine the meaning. For instance, if students focus on the card at the bottom left of the page, with the giant S that appears to be cracking under its own weight, they might say that the heavy S signals that the designer is under pressure or might crack or that she is uncomfortable with her own height. Students can read these elements in relation to the other compositional choices on the card to understand the purpose of each design.

Respond.

1. This assignment asks students to design their own business cards. Start by asking students to note what kind of information they would normally find on a business card (name, address, phone, etc.). What other features do they usually see on a business card? logos? decorative graphics? What about size and shape? (If students want to follow a typical style for business card sizes, you can tell them to make one that is 3 inches by 2.5 inches.) Once you have a list of the business card conventions, students should decide whether they want to follow these conventions or whether they want to stray from them for some reason. Most important: they need to decide what they want the cards to "say" about themselves, and for what purpose. What fonts and graphics will best reflect their personalities?

Students sometimes feel stuck with the business card genre, believing they have to make up a business name in order for the card to make sense. Encourage them to think of this assignment as if they were mak-

ing calling cards, as members of the Victorian upper class used to introduce themselves to others. Depending on their intended audience, they
may decide to include—or leave off—certain information. If they do
not want strange people calling them at home, they may wish to include their email address or instant messenger name but not their home
phone number.

2. This assignment asks students to remove themselves as the subject of
   the card and to practice their audience analysis skills by creating a card
   for an organization with which they are involved. Perhaps they belong
   to a fraternity or sorority that could use business cards with the house
   address on them for alumni mailings, or maybe their religious group
   needs cards to promote a yearly raffle. Suggest that they choose a
   group or organization that could actually *use* the cards they create.
   That way, they can get feedback from the group about whether the
   card meets their needs.

3. This assignment asks students to collect several business cards and to
   analyze the rhetorical effectiveness of one. Writing their response to
   the owner of the card will help students think about how to give con-
   structive feedback to a real audience. You might bring in some cards to
   share with them.

Picture This

This is a somewhat longer assignment, requiring students to gather materials, write, and design a scrapbook about their school for an audience for
prospective students. The first part of this assignment asks them to write
about their personal experiences at the school and to illustrate their writing
with visuals or other mementos representative of their time in school.

The second part of the assignment, in which students gather their materials in a group, will help them edit the scrapbook for their audience. They
will also need to organize the book in some way. For instance, they could
organize the items according to a chronology, or a daily schedule. Perhaps a
thematic approach would work—excitement about being at school, home-
sickness, fitting in, making friends.

The third section asks students to arrange visually the elements on the pages. At this point, you may want them to think about what medium their scrapbook will be—hard copy, so there is one for everyone to share? electronic copy, so that future students can access it online? CD-ROM, so a physical product can be mailed to new students? something else? No matter what medium they choose, at this point your students will need to decide how to put all of the materials they want onto the page, screen, or frame.

They will need to decide as a group how to unify the pages, screens, or frames of their scrapbook. Maybe they will want to include the school's emblem or mascot on each page, or to use the school colors on each page to unify all the disparate elements.

Finally, they need to decide on a title and present the book for viewing to the rest of the class—and perhaps to administrators and other teachers. If your school has an open house coming up, you might try to show it there to prospective students to see their reaction and to get their feedback.

Context and Questions for the Gallery of Images

1. *Three Self-Portraits*. Mixed media by Art Paul, 1993–97. Art Paul was the original art director for *Playboy* magazine and the creator of the *Playboy* bunny logo. For over a year, he created a self-portrait a day in his studio. These daily portraits combine images and words to convey his witty and poignant reflections on life and are as varied as each day was. How do the pose, style and content of the words and the use of color affect the meaning each self-portrait conveys?

2. *American Farm Family on Porch*. Photo by Jack Leigh. Leigh's work records the people, the environment, and the lifestyles of the contemporary American South. His photographs are characterized by a cool candidness; there are no obvious photographic tricks, and we are unaware of the photographer's presence. In many family portraits, conscious posing and staging take place, but Leigh allows the natural family dynamic to emerge on its own. What does the casual but symmetrically balanced composition of this photograph say about the relationships and personalities of the family members?

3. *Men in Park, Peoria, Illinois.* Photo by Arthur Rothstein, 1938. This photo of the dozing men in a park was obviously taken without their knowledge. The photographer had the time to compose his image and crop it in order to emphasize the relaxed, curved gestures of his figures. Note how many curves are used in his image and how they direct the viewer's eyes. How does this unify the image? What overall tone is created by the use of the curves?

4. *Japanese Protestors.* Photo by Agence France—Presse. Just as we are concerned about privacy issues when our lives are made visible, so too are we concerned when our individual lives are made invisible by categorization and government standardization. On August 5, 2002, Japan put into operation a national computerized registry of its citizens. Under the mandatory system, each citizen has an eleven-digit number for online identification by the government. In protesting the new system, these young men used various visual cues to convey their argument— prison stripes; bar codes; a figure from *The Scream*, the painting by Edward Munch; numbers along with the words WE ARE NOT NUMBERS. How do graphics articulate their message differently than words could? How could they get their message across with words?

5. *Home Girl #1.* Painting by Daniel Galvez, 1983. Lowriders are cut-down, dressed-up cars, usually from the 1950s. To make the bond between driver and automobile perfectly clear, owners are also known as lowriders. This portrait of a woman lowrider modifies the photographic convention of a man standing in front of his car by placing the car on the front of the woman. What other compositional choices does the painter make to create a narrative about lowriding?

6. *Daguerreotype and Drawing of Emily Dickinson.* 1893, 1897. Asked at age thirty-one to supply a photograph of herself, the poet Emily Dickinson replied, "Could you believe me—without? I had no portrait, now, but am small, like the Wren, my hair is bold, like the Chestnut Bur— and my eyes, like the sherry in the glass, that the guest leaves—would this do just as well?" Shying from public view, Dickinson chose to represent herself in words rather than in an image. She left behind only an oil portrait, a silhouette, and a daguerreotype made before she turned

twenty. Her family found these images inadequate and commissioned several modified versions that softened her hair, enlarged her eyes, and in some cases added lace trim to her dress, all in order to create a "less severe" image of the poet. If you were Dickinson's publisher, which representation would you use as an author portrait? Which is the most compelling representation, and why? Which would satisfy your need as reader to "see" what Emily Dickinson looked like?

7. *Untitled (Prefer, Refuse, Decide).* By Lorna Simpson. Simpson's work combines words and photographs to create visual narratives that are both literal and suggestive. She is interested in issues of race and gender and the notion of "invisibility." She uses her own body as the model but crops out her facial features or faces away from the camera in order to move away from making an autobiographical statement. By repeating images and words and by then breaking the pattern, she conveys specific meanings. What issue does Simpson examine in the text shown here? What methods does she use to convey her ideas?

4 representing others

This chapter shifts from the personal texts in Chapter 3 to texts that represent others, challenging students to focus on issues such as the perspective a photographer uses when taking photos of people or cultural events, or the point of view that a writer takes when chronicling groups or people different than the writer. Looking at photographs of families, students examine compositional choices such as emphasis, pattern, and unity, and how such elements help us to read the images—what they say, and why. This chapter discusses the problems of stereotyping, and looks in particular at the way texts represent others in historical contexts (including wanted posters and mug shots), cultural contexts (such as travel writing and images), and humorous contexts (noting the subtle distinction between using stereotypes for humor or ill-will in cartoons). The introduction ends with some questions to help students think about the way they represent groups different from their own context—historically, socially, and culturally.

Snapshot

The assignment on page 247 is meant to help students think about how they represent others in their own writing, asking them to study a snapshot they have taken or found and think about why they like it. Although many of us would like to think we represent everyone as they would want to be represented, this is a difficult prospect and, for students, will depend on how much they know about any person they photograph (or write about). If students do not have access to travel photos, bring in some of yours or ones from magazines such as *National Geographic* or *Travel & Leisure*. Additionally, they could search online for travelogs that have photos in them. Here are some search terms students can use to find such texts: "travelogue," "travelog," "travel blog," "travel memoir," "vacation diary," and "trip diary." The textbook's Web site <www.picturingtexts.com> also includes some links to travel photos.

JOSEPH BATHANTI, "Your Mum and Dad"

This is an essay about the writer's parents visiting him and his family. Although this text uses words to convey meaning, the author creates detailed pictures of his parents with those words.

Focus.

1. This question asks the students to compare Bathanti's parents with their own, and to think about how they would represent their parents in a similar piece. How would they describe them? Ask students to choose a detail or two from the story that reminds them of something they have seen their own family members do or say. Does Bathanti fairly represent his parents in the story? What other details (pulling, perhaps, from their own experiences with older family members) might Bathanti have included to make his representation more or less kind?

2. This question asks students to discuss how they are similar to someone in their family and to track how their feelings about that person might have changed over time. They may be able to think of several family members they are like. For instance, they may look exactly like their grandmother but may have the personality of their father while also having the stubborn streak of their aunt. Ask them if they remember the first time they realized these similarities. Do other family members represent these people in similar or different ways? Does their mother describe their maternal grandmother in the same ways as their father?

What can they determine about the way in which their family represents others?

3. This question asks students to consider what Bathanti's parents look like and why he didn't include a photo. Start this question by asking students to write a short description of Bathanti's parents. Have them include descriptors such as height, weight, clothing style, hair color and style, and voice tone. Then, have students share their descriptions with the class. Did they come up with similar or radically different descriptions? Have them look back at their writing and consider whether there is someone they know who looks like the person they described. Perhaps they based their description on one of their own grandparents or on a picture they have seen.

Respond.

1. This exercise asks students to write a caption for a photo so that it represents more about the person than the photo alone can show. Perhaps the student knows the context in which the photo was taken and can write a caption that explains this setting to audiences.

2. For this assignment, students will write an essay about one of their relatives, focusing on a specific trait or incident. Make sure to have them focus on one particular trait or incident and to answer the "so what?" question: Why did this trait or incident have an impact on his or her life and what does it mean to him or her? Students are also asked to provide a photograph of the person they are writing about. In workshopping these essays, have students consider how the photo contributes to the idea they are writing about in the essay. Does the photo need a caption?

3. This assignment asks students to use typefaces and image manipulation software to compose a study of a family member. They will need to know how to scan in photos or to import them from a digital camera. Once they have a photo in Photoshop or a similar program, show them how to create words over the photo—in most programs, by clicking on the Type Tool, represented by a capital A or T in the toolbar, and then

clicking in the place they want the written text to appear. Remind students to choose a typeface and size that appropriately represent the family member as they write about that person. Students can also change the color of their words (usually with a tool called the Color Palette, or as a function within the Type menu) and move them around the page with a Move tool (usually located at the top of the Tool Palette and indicated by a crosshair cursor). In some programs, written text does not wrap, so tell students to break their lines by hitting Return/Enter.

Duane Michals, "A Letter from My Father"

This text shows a photo of a father, mother, and son accompanied by a short, handwritten text about how the father has "hidden his love" from the son.

Focus.

1. This exercise asks students to focus on the facial expressions in the photo, to determine what the narrative might be without reading the written text. You may want to show this photo in class, with the written text covered up. One question asks the students to decide who is "speaking" even though none of the subjects in the photo has his or her mouth open. They may, however, decide that the father is speaking because of his stance. (Ask them how many times they have been lectured by their parents as they hold the same stance.) Ask them what other clues the stances of the subjects give to explain the narrative. Suggest that the two stances are different in emphasis—we see the father's full front, while the son is in profile.

2. This question prompts students to think about metaphor by interpreting Michals's choice of a brick background. Ask students what brick symbolizes to them. Where have they seen brick? What does it feel like? When is brick used? Why would Michals choose brick instead of, say, a sliding-glass door or a window with a lace curtain?

3. This question builds on the previous two questions, asking students to determine the meaning of the entire text based on the individual elements—stance of the subjects, lighting (is it dark or light? how does the lighting relate to our metaphorical and cultural understandings of good/bad?), the brick wall, and so on. Ask students how the written text relates to what the photo says. Do they match? Are there contrasts? Does the verbal text offer additional meaning that we cannot get from the photo itself? What does the typeface say about the son? (Perhaps the photo shows that the relationship between the father and son is frozen in harshness, but the written words suggest that there are kinder moments between them, even if they are unspoken.)

4. This question asks students to look at the mother as she is pictured in the photo to determine how proportion works to suggest more about the family dynamic. Ask students if they noticed her the first time they saw the photo. If not, what does that say about the photo's emphasis?

Respond.

1. This exercise asks students to put themselves in the place of the "other" by taking on the persona of the father or mother and writing a new caption for the photo. They can also change the typeface of their new caption and discuss how a decorative, script, or traditional serif typeface changes the statement made by the caption and photo.

2. In this assignment, students will explore how narratives change as images in a sequence are rearranged. You may want to come to class with photocopies of the example photos shown on page 264. Demonstrate to students by using one of the examples (or one of your own) how placing the three photos on a piece of paper at different intervals changes how our eyes follow the "action" or sequence of the photos. For instance, if the photos are placed at opposite corners of the page, Western audiences typically read from left to right, top to bottom; so, we would see the photos in that order (unless a photo had a visual element that made it stand out from the rest, such as an out-of-proportion or brightly colored element). Or, if we placed the three photos on three

pieces of paper and read them one at a time, we might understand the narrative differently.

HELEN E. STARKWEATHER, "Crisis at Central High"

This text is about a famous photo of the attempted integration of Central High School in Little Rock, Arkansas, in 1957, and the reunion of the two subjects of the photo in 1997, forty years later.

Focus.

1. This exercise asks students to study the details of the 1957 photo and to think about what visual elements are most important. Ask students to list what things they see first, and why. For instance, students may say that they notice the white woman shouting at the back of the black woman, who is wearing sunglasses. Why are these two figures the most prominent in the photo? What makes them the most prominent? What are the other people in the photo doing—paying attention, turning their backs—and what does that contribute to the narrative of this photo? Have they seen other, similar photographs? How do they relate this photo to those other photos? What elements help the students classify this photo as a civil rights photo?

2. This one asks students to compare the composition of the 1957 photo with that of the 1997 photo. What similarities do the photos share? What differences? What do those details and their comparisons suggest about the *purpose* of the second photo? How do the actions of the subjects in the second photo help us to see its purpose? What is the historical context for the second photo (the fortieth anniversary event)?

3. This question asks what questions the author left unanswered about the historical context of the photographs. For instance, can the students determine from the text whether the nine black children were able to attend school that day? Can they determine why it took three years for Central High School to attempt integration? Ask students

whether knowing these details would change their understanding of the text. What does leaving these details out mean for readers? Are they necessary for understanding the text?

Respond.

1. This assignment asks students to craft a narrative about a photo they own that depicts a momentous occasion in their lives. Encourage them to choose events that were important to them, and not necessarily to anyone else—they needn't find a photo equal to the one from Central High! For instance, they may choose a high-school graduation photo (perhaps they were the first high-school graduate of their family?) or one of themselves standing in front of a beat-up car (for which they spent two years working and saving).

2. Students will explore newspapers and magazines in this assignment to find photos that represent current events of this year. Consider starting this assignment by using past examples of current events that marked a year in U.S. history. Like Counts's civil rights photos, you may want to use examples such as the various photos that appeared on magazine covers and newspaper front pages of O. J. Simpson from 1995 or the firefighter photos from 2001 (shown in Chapter 2) and discuss why these are the images that people remember from these years. (Perhaps the *quantity* of reproductions of these images helped emblazon them in popular memory.)

   Students can use online sources of magazines and newspapers, including *Time, Newsweek, The Atlantic,* and the *New York Times* (see <www.picturingtexts.com> for links), or have them use their local newspapers. For online newspapers, students may have to register with their names, addresses, and email accounts, but it is almost always free. Ask students to try to find the image in more than one source, and to see if they can find differing descriptions of the same photos or events in different newspapers and magazines. They should add this information to their analysis of the image—and account for why they think such differences in reporting exist.

Annu Palakunnathu Matthew, "An Indian from India"

This selection shows Matthew, a photographer, dressed up in the kind of exotic garb seen in nineteenth-century photographs of Indians and Native Americans to show British citizens what "foreigners" looked like. Her intention, as she says in the statement that accompanies the photos, is to mimic the representations of the earlier photographs, to question the way all "types" of people are stereotyped.

Focus.

1. This question asks students to look at six key words that Matthew uses—"then and now, us and them, exotic and local"—and to discuss what she means by them. Students may need help understanding the general differences between Indians from India and Native Americans.

Ask students how Matthew's photos compare to the ones of Native Americans taken over a hundred years ago. How has she made the photos look similar? How do the photos lead us to reflect on the "us and them" distinction? Who is "us" and who is "them"? How do Matthew's photos break down those barriers? What becomes "local" in Matthew's representations? (Is anything local?) Why did past generations, or why *do* current generations, consider the original photos "exotic"? What specifics are we given about the three historical photos? How does this lack of contextual information contribute to our generalizations about the people and their culture in those photos?

If you have students of Native American or Indian descent in your class, they may offer more details on their own cultural heritage that can inform the class, but do not expect or require them to do so. If they want to share information about themselves and their cultural history, make sure students are aware that one student's experience may be totally different from another person's from the same tribe. Representing others is a difficult task—which is Matthew's point.

2. This exercise asks how the people represented in Matthew's photo would exoticize *us*. Start this discussion by asking students to consider some stereotypical things people say or think about their age group. List some common complaints—perhaps that they listen to loud music, watch too much TV? Discuss some of the popular media's representations of their age group (in other words, how do people *not* of their generation view them?). For instance, Matthew uses clothing as a way to show difference—what do students wear that might lump them into categories in which they would not necessarily classify themselves? If you have students of different generations in your class, juxtapose how each generation would be represented—a soccer mom, a jock, a punk, whatever. Ask students if they actually *fit* these stereotypes. How would they feel if these were the only representations of themselves that others could see?

Respond.

1. This assignment asks students to compare travel photos with Matthew's photos and to write about how one could take pictures that did not exoticize the people in them. One mistake many novice photographers make when taking pictures of people is not to ask permission. Review some strategies for asking people for permission to take their pictures. Some cultures, such as the Gullah, believe that photography steals souls, so it's crucial to establish the appropriateness of snapping a picture in some cases. If a person agrees to be photographed, it's good to ask what surroundings they would prefer—perhaps they would like to be seen in their home with their possessions, or in the city market, or talking with friends. It is important to focus on the person in his or her larger cultural and social contexts.

2. This assignment is to design a poster presentation showing how students in other countries are represented in school photographs. Students may have difficulty finding pictures of students from other countries, but have them visit <www.picturingtexts.com> for links to sources with such images, as well as information about how to document those sources.

They are also asked to develop a theme for their presentation—this is where they might need help. Suggest that they look for a common theme in the two groups—for example, age, gender, or clothing style. These themes will come out of how the students represent themselves and how they are represented in the photos.

Gina Kolata and Iver Peterson, "New Way to Insure Eyewitnesses Can ID the Right Bad Guy"

This reading indicates that eyewitness identifications of police suspects are notoriously inaccurate and even false, and argues that by viewing a sequence of photos instead of a lineup, eyewitnesses can more accurately identify the person they saw commit a crime.

Focus.

1. This question asks students to reflect on whether or not sequential photo lineups are necessary and to discuss what other factors are at play when audiences read these lineups. One way to discuss this issue in class is to bring in a videotape of a police drama such as *Law & Order* or *NYPD Blue*. Many episodes of these shows incorporate police lineups into the plot and often discuss issues relating to the accuracy of identification, including racial factors, police interference, the witness's emotional or psychological state, and the order of people in a lineup. Show one or more clips in class and ask students to list some of the issues involved in live lineups. They can then relate those issues to sequential photo lineups to see which problems remain and which are ameliorated by the new process.

2. This question asks students to examine if they have ever been stereotyped—as, for instance, a jock, a sorority girl, a returning student, or a bad driver. Would that situation create a problem for them if they appeared in a police lineup?

Respond.

1. This exercise asks students to write a caption for the photo shown on page 280, and to explain why they have written this caption. Ask them what clues in the photo help them to create a caption. What if there were something outside the frame of the picture as it is shown here— say, a lion running after the two men or a flood filling the streets? How would this larger context change their interpretation of and understanding of how these two men are represented?

2. This assignment asks students to create an ad against crime. Start by asking them to list crime issues that concern them, as college students. Have them each, or in groups, choose an issue for their ad. How might they use a visual metaphor or crime-related generic photo or image to help convey the meaning of their message?

Peter Menzel and Charles Mann, "Material World: A Global Family Portrait"

In this selection, students can compare two photographs of families—one from the United States and one from Japan—accompanied by a list of their material possessions, which are prominently featured in the photos.

Focus.

1. This question asks students to discuss what these texts show about households a world apart—one in Texas and one in Japan. Ask them to focus on the photograph and to describe the compositional elements of the people and items. For instance, in the Texas photo, the family (husband, wife, daughter, and son) stands close together in the foreground, the mother holding the family Bible. The Japanese family (husband, wife, and two daughters) sits around the kitchen table in the same line of sight as their possessions. What if anything do these varying perspectives say about the families in the photos?

2. This question asks students to focus on some of the rhetorical choices the designer made. Ask students to focus on the written list that accompanies each photo. To get a sense of what purpose these texts might serve, have students make a list of the items from the Texas household they have in their homes. How many items do they share with the Japanese household? How many does each household have in common? Does the similarity surprise them? Do students consider themselves, or Americans in general, to be an audience for this text?

3. This question asks students to focus on the cultures depicted in these photos. Ask students what is valued—what is emphasized in each photo? For instance, the Texas mom is holding her family Bible, while the Japanese family sits at the dining table drinking from teacups. How do these two presentations—design choices by the photographers—show what is valued in each place?

Respond.

1. This assignment asks students to write a letter to one of the families. They should mention details from the photo they found interesting (and say why) and ask a question or two about the family's life. They should also tell the family something about themselves and include a photo. If they do not have a photo, they should say *what* they would want to show about themselves photographically.

2. This assignment asks students to create their own version of "Material World" based on their own room. If they cannot photograph their rooms, suggest that they draw them. Or they could make a list of the items in their rooms, as is done in the reading. In their written descriptions, remind them to articulate why they have the items they do, not just what they have, and how these possessions reflect on them as a person.

3. This assignment asks students to write an essay about some favorite possession and what it says about them as a person. They will first need to choose their audience. They should have fun with this project, for it allows them to write about something they really like—to explain

why they like it and what it reveals about them. For instance, do they value their stereo equipment? Or love a certain video game? Perhaps they have a collection of teacups—or stuffed flamingoes. Ask students to describe when, why, and/or how they acquired these items and why they are important; remind them that they might want to include a photo *showing* their favorite thing.

Tom Phillips, "The Cards We Choose to Send"

This selection of postcards represents a variety of people, places, and things.

Focus.

1. This exercise would work well done in class as a group discussion, asking students to compare how people are represented in the postcards shown. Start discussion with one of the postcards. Have students look at the card with the two women, and ask them what era they think it is from. They might have difficulty separating the historical and cultural clues of the photo (the popularity of musicals in the 1950s, the women's hairstyles and clothes, the interior design) from the idea that this postcard may not be from the 1950s, but is mimicking the decade for a satirical purpose. From here, you can lead students on to the other postcards.

Although students may not be able to do such in-depth analysis of their cards without some research, you can provide them with starting points, based on the written and visual clues in each postcard.

2. This question asks students to notice the visual composition of the postcards shown here. Have students analyze the composition strategies of one of the cards. For instance, in the postcard of the men in Florida, how does the repetition of the subjects—all in a row, shown from the back—make a statement? And point of view—why do they think the photographer showed these men from the back rather than the front? Metaphorically, what could that framing represent?

3. This question asks students to focus on the written words in the post-cards. The Marilyn postcard may be difficult for students to understand, so beginning discussion with it might be helpful. Ask students to interpret this postcard—some may understand the connection between the name, the candle (a reference to the Elton John song "Candle in the Wind"), and the way the base of the candle appears to hover in midair (resembling the way Marilyn Monroe's skirt flew above her knees in *The Seven-Year Itch*). Then have students cover the name at the bottom of the card and ask them if they would understand the card's purpose without the name.

Respond.

1. This assignment asks students to imagine they've actually visited a place where they bought one of these cards and to write a message to a friend *about* that place. They are to write about the place in positive terms and not to exoticize the people there as they describe them.

2. This assignment asks students to create a postcard showing students at their school, to write a message to friends or family on the back, and then to analyze how their words and design represent the school fairly and accurately. If you do this assignment in class, have students bring in any art supplies they might have. Remind them to think about the many different groups on campus—to represent others as well as themselves in this postcard.

3. This assignment asks students to analyze a song or video for any stereotypical representations and to write a review discussing what they find. One good example to show in class is the *Mikado* rehearsal scene from *Topsy Turvy*, the film about Gilbert and Sullivan, when three Chinese women are being asked to walk downstage so the British women can mimic their movements. Ask students how this clip might represent stereotypical thinking about Chinese women (the British women's caricatured portrayal of what they *think* Chinese women look and act like is a good answer).

Cynthia Selfe and Marilyn Cooper,
"Teo Gets a Brother": A Storybook in Progress

This deliberately unfinished children's story provides a starting point for students to discuss how to talk about discrimination and stereotypes with younger siblings or friends. In the story, Teo's family adopts a boy who does not look like them.

Focus.

1. This question asks students to draw on what they have learned about how images and words work together to tell a story. Try focusing on one spread for this assignment. Begin by pointing out that children's books are typically unified across a two-page spread. Helping students see how two pages can work together as one (with the same color scheme or theme) might help them choose which spread they want to use.

2. Taking what they learn in the preceding question, students research other children's books to discover how these texts use words and images to represent others. It might be useful to ask students to find a children's book with surprising subject matter—perhaps they will discover a book that addresses tough issues, such as sexual orientation, health matters, divorce, or adoption.

Respond.

1. This assignment asks students to write a review of the book about Teo, based on what they think the intended audience and purpose are. In this review, they may want to address what changes (including what ending) they would make to the story and how those changes would impact the story's meaning. Discuss what makes a successful book review: a summary of the book; an analysis of how the book meets its intended audience and purpose (using specific textual references); a mention of what in the book falls short of meeting the needs of its au-

dience, if anything; and a recommendation (or not) to others to read (or not read) the book and why.

2. This assignment asks students to finish the story, keeping in mind that children will be the text's audience. They will need to draw images or use clip art to finish the plot they write. Ask them to consider *how* they want the story to end. Based on what they learned in this chapter, what ending seems appropriate? How might they add more suspense to the story? After they have a draft of their story, it might be useful for them to have some children read it (their cousins, younger siblings, or friends' kids). If your school has a childcare program, this might be a good place to test the story.

3. This assignment asks students to revise their story for a different age group. The first item to focus on is who students want the audience to be. Then, they will need to decide how to change the elements of the story—illustrations, plot, word choice—to match their new audience. This assignment provides an opportunity to explore genres such as young adult literature, teenage romance novels, or others. It might be interesting to ask them to revise the story *without* pictures.

4. This assignment asks students to revise their story, this time for the original age group of children three to six years old. Have students work in small groups, each revising the story including fonts, images, and wording that will be easily understood by the intended audience. When students are done, have them compare their choices during a class session where they read each other's work. How different are the versions? Why?

CHRISTOPHER HART, "How to Draw Comic Book Heroes and Villains"

This selection consists of two examples from a book on how to draw comic book characters—good girls, bad guys, and so on.

Focus.

1. This exercise asks students to reflect on the historical stereotypes of Jubilee. Ask them what stereotypical cultural themes they see in her written profile and pictorial depiction. Note, for instance, references to her family, their economic status, and her schooling.

2. This question challenges students to think of any comic book characters that do not depend on stereotypes. Students may be familiar with the *X-Men* characters, many of whom have disabilities that they use as powers (although scholars in disability studies say that these examples are problematic). Ask students to bring in examples. Alternatively, have them watch a clip from a live-action movie that features a character from comics—*Superman*, *Spiderman*, or *X-Men*—and discuss in class what traits the character has in common with those listed on page 248 and what traits are not common to stereotypical characters.

Respond.

1. This assignment asks students to write a profile of a favorite superhero or villain. Students may want to use print comics, or they could refer to DC Comics or Marvel Comics's Web site (see <www.picturingtexts.com> for links). (Or they could search on "comics" and see what other resources they can find.) Many of these online sources have pictures of the characters that students can use as examples when writing their profiles. Make sure students describe the background of their character as well as his or her superpowers.

2. This assignment asks students to create their own nonstereotypical superhero or villain. Ask them if they have ever thought about a superpower that would be useful and how they might be able to accompany that with a character who does not have stereotypical traits. They might remember Inspector Gadget, the bumbling detective who could do amazing feats with spring-loaded shoes and a helicopter hat.

Students are then asked to take on the role of editor, helping another writer revise his or her superhero. What suggestions do they have?

Does the character seem likable (or not likable, if she or he is a villain)? Are any of the character's traits *not* stereotypical?

Picture This

This project asks students to analyze the way their school represents the student body in its official publications. They will need to research demographic statistics at their school—typically the office of records and registration or the registrar's office (wherever students go to enroll in or apply to the school) will list these statistics on its Web site or in a brochure. Students may have to dig a bit to find this information, but all schools should make it available. Using these statistics, students can compare the actual student populations to the population as it is represented in the school's promotional materials. Remind them that they will need to document which publications they use for the photos and the statistics.

To help students get started, you might have them read the article by Jennifer Jacobson about the University of Wisconsin's problematic brochure, on p. 340.

Context and Questions for the Gallery of Images

1. *Woman Wrapped in Cloth.* Photo by Colin Anderson/Corbis.
   This photo presents a contemporary interpretation of the veiled woman. How does this image compare with others of veiled women?

2. *Mother Simeon Shooting Snooker, Tyburn Convent.* Photo by Shannon Taggart, 1998.
   This photo's charm and tension come from showing nuns in a way that we don't usually think of them. Strong diagonal lines along with interesting light and shadow create a dynamic composition, one that draws us in. How does this photo compare with other photos of nuns?

3. *India's Future Looks to Its Past.* Photo by Agence France-Press.
   In Lucknow, India, 133 children dressed like Mohandas Gandhi to celebrate the anniversary of his birth. Gandhi was a spiritual leader who espoused nonviolent change. Compare this photo to the one of the child dressed like Elvis that appears on page 310 of the textbook.

4. *Elvis Day, 2002.* This photo of two-year-old Madelyn Berzon was taken on Elvis Day at the childcare center she attends in Ellisville, Missouri. When the center sent home a color photo of Madelyn dressed up like Elvis, the background (a schoolroom) did not seem to represent the right era, so Madelyn's mom digitally replaced it with this background of a diner and gas station. Since the new background was black and white, she then made the whole image black and white. Are there any clues in the photo that help you tell the child's image is superimposed on the background? (The yellow haze around her is one clue.)

5. *Little Girls with Their Dolls and Buggies, Caldwell, Idaho.* Photo by Russell Lee, 1941.
   Taken for the Farm Security Administration, this documentary photograph reflects life in America at the time—but for what audience, and what groups?

6. *Pro-Choice Public Education Project.* Ad by DeVito/Verdi Ad Agency.
   The format of this ad was inspired by the art of Barbara Kruger, who looks to advertising for her inspiration. What significance does the background image have in relation to the words in the ad?

7. From *Postcards from Camp.* Painting by Ben Sakoguchi.
   This imagined picture postcard depicts life in the internment camps where Japanese Americans were sent during World War II (and where the artist spent his early childhood). The painting includes Sakoguchi's own family photos as well as archival images and quotations from government agencies. The words at the bottom were of course not written to be a caption for this image. How do they affect the way audiences see the image?

8. *Harlem.* Photo by James VanDerZee; *Negro Women near Earle, Arkansas,* photo by Dorothea Lange, 1936.
   VanDerZee chronicled the Harlem Renaissance in New York City during the 1920s and 1930s, while Lange documented life in the United States for the Works Progress Administration. Compare the poses and composition of VanDerZee's photo to those of Lange's.

5 constructing realities

This chapter is divided into four sections: Picturing Reality, Interpreting Reality, Envisioning Unseen Realities, and Creating Realities.

The Picturing Reality section focuses on the issues of digitally manipulating images to change, distort, or enhance their meaning. Several examples are given, including a University of Wisconsin brochure in which an African American student was added to a photo of white students at a football game.

In the Interpreting Reality section, students are made aware of how both authors and designers choose to include or leave out detail of texts, as when we include snapshots of certain people in our family photo albums while leaving others out.

In Envisioning Unseen Realities, students are reminded how microscopes helped scientists first picture natural elements that were otherwise too small for humans to see. Although this technology helped us advance scientifically, scientists also *alter* these images to create "better" or more understandable pictures, as when they doctor an image with color to create a clear distinction between microscopic or telescopic images that nonscientists might not otherwise understand.

In Creating Realities, students are asked to explore gaming and created environments such as *The Matrix* and *The Sims* in order to examine how these worlds are created to appear "real."

The chapter ends by reminding students that although texts such as photographs have long been held up as "truth," they have been *constructed* by someone for some purpose.

Snapshot

This exercise on page 331 asks students to review pictures, especially group photos, they have taken of friends and family to determine how the photo's composition mediates what we see. Begin discussion by asking them to describe the context in which their photo was taken.

KENNETH BROWER, "A Flock of Golden Retrievers"

This reading examines how nature photographers differ in their opinions about digitally manipulating photos for public consumption. Two photographers' work is detailed: Galen Rowell, who believes that changing any element of a photo through digital image manipulation is not ethical, and Art Wolfe, who doctors photos by adding animals that were not actually present.

Focus.

1. This question asks students to examine closely the examples in this reading and to determine connections between the ethical choices Rowell makes and those of other nature photographers. It might help to write a list on the board of each artist's examples (you would have two categories, Rowell and Wolfe). Ask students to discuss what they think accounts for the differing ethical standards of these two photographers. For instance, Wolfe's photos involve manipulations of subject matter, including adding more elephants or zebras or cheetah cubs. The photos Rowell took, which were also manipulated, involved *not* the changing of subject matter, but instead the changing of positions so that an image would fit on a magazine cover or within other parameters, as in the case of the picture for the cover of *Mountain Light* (see paragraph 10). Point out the different publication venues for these photos—Rowell's are for books he published or for personal use (such as the bald eagle photo, which was never published) while Wolfe's are for publications such as *National Geographic*, whose audiences might expect their pho-

tos to be "realistic," not manipulated to create an appealing visual (as in the case of the polar bear picture).

2. This question asks students to think about the Dalai Lama's statement that photographs can tell the truth about experiences *if* the person who took the photo is a reliable source, and to apply this statement to the situation in which Senator Joseph McCarthy used photos to discredit his foes. You may need to tell students about McCarthy's political history regarding communism or have them do research on how he used photos. Ask students if they trust their current Congressional representatives or the presidency to tell the truth. You may need to explain the cultural contexts surrounding today's presidency versus those in the 1940s and 1950s.

Respond.

1. This question asks students to find a thesis sentence in Brower's article that explains the ethics of digital manipulation. Students might decide that there are several places in the article that sum up Brower's argument about ethics. Some that are good candidates include paragraph 4, which narrates the story of people's disappointment upon hearing that the brown bear photograph on Rowell's wall is a fake. Or see paragraph 23, where the joy of seeing a wonderful event in action is displaced by people's reactions to learning that a photo is fake. Perhaps the most succinct thesis statement in this article is in paragraph 6: "Even as images grow sharper with digital enhancement, the honest path grows murkier, and Rowell feels that students need guidance." You might require students to reread the article closely, looking for the sentence or two they believe holds the argument; or let them know they need to look for the thesis statement before they read the article.

2. This assignment asks students to digitally manipulate an image using software. If you have access to a scanner or digital camera, you may want to bring it to class. If students want to try Wolfe's methods, with multiple objects repeating through a single image, they may try making several copies of one image (or duplicating layers with that image) and

moving the subject of that image to different areas of the frame. There are several tools in programs such as Photoshop or ImageComposer that can help students create duplicates of images or parts of images.

3. This assignment asks students to analyze the Tourist of Death photos that abounded on the Web after September 11, 2001. They will need to determine the audience and purpose of photos such as these. Students can write about other Internet hoaxes as well; <www.Snopes.com> is a good resource for examples. This assignment can lead into a discussion about the use of the Internet as a cultural image-manipulation and circulation tool. Ask students if they have ever received a joke or chain letter email that seemed like a hoax. What have they done about it? Did they forward it when the sender asked them? Did they delete it? If so, why? Have they ever received the same hoax email more than once, from different people? How could they find out if it was a hoax? (Refer back to what the Dalai Lama said about Extremely Hidden Phenomena and see if students can apply that knowledge to the person who sent such email.) How does their experience with email hoaxes help them to understand the audiences that spread images such as Tourist of Death?

JENNIFER JACOBSON, "In Brochures, What You See Isn't Necessarily What You Get"

This reading examines the controversy that arose when the University of Wisconsin placed the face of an African American student into a group photo of white students at a football game that they then used on a brochure for prospective students. Accurately portraying diversity on campus can play a large role in why such manipulation is done, even if the manipulation itself is perceived as unethical.

Focus.

1. This question asks students to look at the decisions they made (and the publication materials they referred to) when deciding to attend their

school. Have students refer to the publications of their school to see how it portrays different groups of people. Do its brochures, flyers, and Web sites give an accurate view of who's on campus? Do they recognize the groups the students belong to or not?

2. This question asks students to discuss whether doctoring images to include underrepresented groups is any different ethically than asking students from each group to pose for photos. This question can prompt much discussion in class. You may want to ask students to reflect further on what Jacobson says is the de facto segregation of social and cultural groups on campus. Ask if it would be possible for a photographer on their campus to photograph a group of their friends and have it represent the diversity of the student population. Do they socialize with many people who are different from themselves ethnically?

If your school is very diverse, ask students to think about schools where the population is mostly one ethnic or racial group. Students may be unfamiliar with schools that mark themselves by their race, including Historically Black Colleges and Universities (HBCUs) such as Howard or Spelman. Ask students to collect a number of Web site images or brochures from a range of schools, including HBCUs, land-grant universities, community colleges, and schools with religious affiliations, such as Bob Jones University. Have them examine the photos of students used in these publications to see how they do or do not represent the likely populations of the schools. Would those images prompt them to attend that school? Why or why not?

Respond.

1. This assignment asks students to look closely at the student population on their own campus. While they may already have analyzed the printed publications for the school, this project asks them to photograph the student population from a specific location. You may want students to work in groups, or have each student sign up for a specific location, to cover as many spots as possible on campus. Or, if you have access to a digital camera or can provide a disposable camera, have stu-

dents use it over the course of one day, all at the same central location to document the student population that passes by. Documenting three or four spots on campus over several hours might present an interesting representation of the student body. Have students discuss in class a good spot from which to photograph—they probably know the best spots and the most heavily trafficked areas.

2. This assignment asks students to think about a family photograph and to write an essay explaining why the image does or does not reflect their real, lived experience of the moment. For instance, they might want to write about a photo from a religious holiday such as Chanukah, Ramadan, or Christmas. Does the photo detail everything about that occasion that they remember? If not, how does it differ? Perhaps the photo shows relatives who are smiling while, in reality, they were arguing about how to make dinner.

3. This assignment asks students to write an essay about the ethics of representation that may distort reality. Students could focus on the Wisconsin brochure conflict, in which case they may want to learn more about affirmative action. Or, they could choose another image-manipulation ethical dilemma, such as when fashion magazines change the way photographs of models look.

KATE BETTS, "The Man Who Makes the Pictures Perfect"

This reading examines the role Pascal Dangin, a celebrated photo retoucher, plays in the beauty and fashion industry—and how his images affect the self-esteem of those of us whose bodies do not resemble the ones we see in fashion magazines.

Focus.

1. This question asks students to discuss Dangin's claim that retouching is ethically fine. Start by asking what magazines they read. How many of

those are fashion/beauty magazines or health magazines that focus on physical appearance? Why do they read them? Also, ask students to name a movie star whom they would like to look like. How would they react if they discovered that their favorite photo of that star was doctored to make him or her look twenty pounds lighter or ten years younger? What about having family photos retouched to make their mother look younger? Their grandmother?

2. This question asks students to discuss when and why it would be appropriate to alter a photograph. You might begin by discussing genre. Bring in several examples of photos from a local newspaper—news, fashion, food, and feature photos. If possible, manipulate each photo to distort its intention. For instance, you could change an important detail in a news photo by moving it or redesigning it so that the students will question which version (the original or the manipulated one) is accurate. Or, in a food photo, change the colors of the food (in Photoshop, for example, you can typically adjust the hue and saturation of colors). Show students both photos at once and ask them to determine which one is a "true" representation of the original subject and whether the manipulated version is ethically sound or not.

Respond.

1. This assignment is to write an essay that examines the connections between fashion images and eating disorders. Students may want to focus on models or on the audience for these ads. This essay is an opportunity for them to research the cultural implications of the fashion industry. Perhaps they may also want to include a personal narrative in their essay, of a time when they or someone they knew remarked on their body size. You may need to encourage male students in the class to explore how this issue relates to men, considering that much literature focuses this issue on women.

2. This assignment asks students to analyze the promotion of health and physical beauty in men's health magazines. You may want to expand this assignment and ask students to go to a library or store and write

down the titles of articles on the covers of men's and women's magazines that relate to diet, beauty, and health. Have them keep a description of the kinds of models who appear on the covers with these titles. Another genre of magazine they may want to explore is cooking magazines—how do the article titles on the cover compare with cover photographs? (Often, these magazines will discuss low-fat or low-calorie meals while showing a picture of a frosted cake.) You could have students work in groups and do a group presentation, including visuals from the magazines, to persuade the class to heed or ignore (or take with a grain of salt) the given advice.

David Quammen, "The Boilerplate Rhino"

This reading tracks the history of how the rhinoceros has been visually portrayed and how we assume that nature is represented accurately in nature videos and shows—and what impact such secondhand visual representations have on our understanding of nature.

Focus.

1. This question asks students to focus on the written text to determine the author's tone. If students have trouble determining the tone, try reading passages or assign parts for students to read aloud (give them time to review the essay as homework before asking them to read aloud so that they can ask you questions about its tone). Ask them how the written text conveys tone—what kind of diction, word patterns, and organization does Quammen use? From what viewpoint does he write, and for what audience? For instance, in the first paragraph, he writes in the second-person—*you*—which is often used in written texts to imply that the writer knows what the audience is doing (or should be doing). It can be a presumptuous tone. Ask if the students felt the writer was talking directly to them, and how that affected their reading of the essay. Have they ever watched a nature video, and if so, did they believe the animals were accurately represented? How does

this relate to Quammen's turn from Dürer back to Blockbuster's nature videos?

2. This question requires students to identify in the essay what made it possible for Dürer's woodcut to gain international fame. If they have difficulty finding an answer, point them to paragraph 10. You may want to give them some history of the printing press and information about how knowledge was transmitted before multiple copies were possible.

Respond.

1. This assignment asks students to think about nature videos and how their medium of publication changes their purpose. You may want to refer students to the discussion of publication outlets in the reading "A Flock of Golden Retrievers." One way to approach this assignment in class is to break students into small groups and have each group brainstorm the audience and purpose for a different medium and genre of nature video, such as the examples given in the textbook — *The Crocodile Hunter*, National Geographic *Explorer*, and IMAX films.

Or, if possible, have students videotape or bring in videotapes of shows that appear on the National Geographic and Animal Planet cable channels. Both channels offer programming focused on animals. Have them analyze the audience and purpose for each channel's shows. Does one channel offer more diverse animal programming? Do some shows seem intentionally realistic or more manipulated? For instance, if students look at the prime-time programming on Animal Planet, they might find an exaggerated wild-animal show such as *Crocodile Hunter*, a game show such as *Pet Stars*, or a drama such as *Animal Cops*. How do these shows compare to the seemingly more realistic portrayal of wild animals on National Geographic?

2. This assignment asks students to compare Dürer's woodcut with a photo of a rhino — both shown on the opening spread of this reading. Students are then asked to search online for information about rhinos.

A simple search on "rhinoceros" will yield hundreds of thousands of sites. There are several links on <www.picturingtexts.com> that students can use to search more accurately. Or bring in printouts of rhino research you have done and have students compare the information about rhino behavior with the descriptions Dürer gave. How accurate was Dürer?

3. This assignment asks students to write an essay analyzing a travel video about a place they have visited. Because not all students have had the chance to travel (or to rent a video about that place), another way to approach this assignment is to contact your local Chamber of Commerce or Visitor's Information Center to find a video promoting the area in which the school is located or to contact the publications department on campus to get a recruitment video about the school. This way, all students will have some knowledge about the places mentioned in the video. Usually these videos are short, so it may be possible to view one in class.

Vicki Goldberg, "Even Scientific Images Have Trouble Telling the Truth"

This reading focuses on how scientists enhance images and photographs so that laypeople are better able to see the points the scientist wants the visual to make. Goldberg also discusses how some scientific images differ depending on how or when they are photographed—the Crab Nebula, for example, looks different depending on the means used to photograph it.

Focus.

1. This question asks students to analyze each of the Crab Nebula pictures using the key terms given in Chapter 1. Students may notice, for example, that the first image is scattered, with a consistent emphasis throughout the frame, while the second is unified with emphasis in the

center of the frame. This makes the second figure resemble what audiences may be used to recognizing as a star or planet cluster.

2. This question asks students to examine their cultural and social understandings of colors. You might bring in texts that contain colors with strong North American cultural associations although the subjects of the texts are from other countries. For example, a stop sign from France is red but is not the same shape as ours and does not have the words STOP or ARRETE on it. Or, to show different cultural understandings of color, bring in a photograph of a red wedding dress from China and have students discuss their understanding of it. You may want to refer to a cultural color association chart, such as the one on the Witchita University Psychology Department Web site (see <www.picturingtexts.com>).

Respond.

1. This assignment asks students to think about the relationship between art and science, based on the coloration of the molecular makeup of several drinks. Is colorizing scientific visuals unethical? You may want students to look on the Web site for information about these images and discuss their purpose—why were these images colorized? What are they being used for now?

2. This assignment asks students to analyze a scientific article in a newspaper to determine what the audience needs to know about the topic in order to understand it and to consider how the significance of a scientific discovery is communicated. Students can find scientific articles online, in any number of places including national or international newspapers (they may have to register for free before accessing the article's text) or on Web sites such as NASA's.

You may want to ask students to choose a scientific discovery from the last ten years and have them find an article about the discovery in more than one publication for the sake of comparison. For instance, if students want to research the mapping of the human genome, they will find many articles about its progress, as well as independent Web sites, including the Celera Web site. This could be a class project in which small groups of students examine one or two kinds of publications, and then they can come together to write segments of their own Web site (or a linked essay) describing their findings and analyzing the different accounts given by each publication or author.

David Brooks, "Oversimulated Suburbia"

This reading is about the popularity of the role-playing computer game *The Sims*, in which players choose characters that they then feed, clothe, and socialize—and for whom they "construct" homes that they then furnish and "upgrade." Culturally, the game reflects what many of us do in everyday life—try to keep up with, if not exceed, the Joneses.

Focus.

1. This exercise asks students to analyze the tone Brooks uses in his article. In paragraph 9, for example, Brooks uses six exclamation points, as well as diction that resembles spoken language. He relies on second-person address, telling the audience what they should find exciting—"authentic Victorian wallpaper" and "pet gyms." Notice how he quotes a Sims player who seems as exuberant about the game as Brooks is. Ask students to read the paragraph aloud and then describe what emotions Brooks might be trying to represent with his choice of punctuation and diction.

2. This question asks students to classify themselves according to the two categories Brooks gives for Sims players: social and materialistic. Ask students if they think these classifications are fair. Can they categorize themselves this way? What do these basic definitions leave out? If students have not played *The Sims*, they can go online and search on "The Sims" to discover the range of Web sites devoted to promoting the

health and well-being, as well as financial and material stability, of these characters. The question also asks how similar we are to Sims players—ask students whether they purchase any of the same stuff that Sims players do for their Sims characters.

3. This question asks students to think about what function Sims stories serve. Brooks relates these stories to a "cultural landscape in which *Oprah* meets *Friends, Terms of Endearment*, and *MTV's Real World.*" You might ask students why they think he draws this analogy—what does each of these shows or movies tell us about our current "cultural landscape"? What is their function? Students may think of this form of writing as therapy—by writing the story of an abusive situation, the writer is able to acknowledge that situation (and perhaps read other, similar examples). However, remind them that fiction is just that—fictive. What purpose might the author of such stories have for writing about a fictive situation?

Respond.

1. This question asks students to chart the reality level of reality TV shows and videogames. For a full listing of reality shows and video-games, see <www.picturingtexts.com>. One Web site, *Reality TV Links*, lists over one hundred reality shows. Have students group these shows into categories such as Adventure (which might include programs such as *Survivor* and video games such as *Quake*). Students can work in groups to chart the shows and games in each category, creating a class-wide chart.

Using this chart, students can write about why reality programs and games are more or less real. What are the criteria for "real"? Do the graphics in video games have to be 3-D and very detailed? Do TV programs in which the "actors" address the camera (such as *The Real World*) feel more or less real than those shows where the actors do not break the fourth wall (such as *Queer Eye for the Straight Guy*)?

2. This assignment asks students to write an essay analyzing the attraction of creating an alternate self in a game like *The Sims*. Students may

be able to imagine endless freedom in such games, but remind them that they are constructing realities in doing so and that video games do not offer endless opportunities, even if they seem to. For instance, *The Sims* promotes social formations, including sexual relationships and marriage partners, but at least the early versions did not offer the option of same-sex partners. Students may have seen similar options overlooked in this or other games, such as not being able to pair a hairstyle they want with the skin color they choose.

Picture This

This assignment asks students to create an advertisement to promote a group to which they belong, and, in doing so, to think about publication venue and audience. This project challenges them to construct an accurate representation of their group using both verbal and visual texts. Tell students they can use various genres and media—for example, magazine ad, poster, or commercial. If you have access to digital technology, encourage students to use it. Refer students to Chapter 7 for more help with design choices for print publications. Encourage them to work with one or two other students on this project. They may be able to use what they produce to promote their group.

Context and Questions for the Gallery of Images

1. *Paris, Eiffel Tower.* Photo contact print by Thomas Kellner. 1977.
Kellner creates photographs consisting of many fragmented views of buildings that are cultural icons. He starts by taking an entire roll of film of the building from different angles and then making a contact print (a proof sheet of single-frame images). The fragmented image that results from this process includes multiple views pieced together to form a whole. How does this method of deconstructing and reassembling a building affect the meaning of a culture icon such as the Eiffel Tower? How do multiple points of view within one image affect your point of view?

2. *Flying Goldfish.* Installation and photo by Sandy Skogland, 1981.
   Skogland's photographs have been described as tableau photography, staged scenes in which the characters do not move or speak. They begin as installations, which she designs, constructs, and stages with figures who assume certain poses and gestures. Her work is often dreamlike, combining naturalism with bizarre colors and objects. This installation is photographed and exhibited simultaneously, causing viewers to reflect on the nature of photographic truth. How does the monochromatic color in the background add to the power of this image? Which parts are based on reality and which parts create an obvious unreality?

3. *London Tube Shop.* Photo by Joel DeGrande.
   Using QuickTime and Photoshop computer programs, DeGrande stitches together photographs taken in precisely calibrated increments to form a complete 360-degree image. This image can then be viewed in QuickTime as a moving image, cropped and flattened into a panoramic photograph as shown here. Time and space are thus combined and compressed into a single moment that is perceived as a snapshot. The image becomes more abstract as it is flattened, as we see simultaneously what is in front of us and behind us. The train on the left side is the same one we see on the right. The two tunnels are actually the same tunnel, with light at one end, darkness at the other. How does DeGrande use pattern and rhythm to achieve a unity of place that helps us believe his constructed reality?

4. *Flight.* Photo by Sam Mapp, 2002.
   Piecing together fifteen slices of two identical photographs, Mapp creates a kinetic photograph—one with movement. He allows the seams to show, showing us how the image was constructed. Mapp thus takes the compressed moment of a single snapshot and with the use of repetition extends time, thereby creating the illusion of movement. The rhythm and pattern in Mapp's photograph are obvious. How do they affect the way you read this image? Is the reality any less convincing than DeGrande's seamless construction? How does the right leg extending off the edge affect the way we read the image?

5. *Seventh Avenue, New York City.* Photograph by Eli Reed, 1986.

   At first glance, Ronald Reagan appears to be standing on Seventh Avenue and actually walking towards us. In fact, he is made of cardboard, though he looks quite real in the midst of the very real pedestrians walking by him. You might say the cardboard figure is a constructed reality—as is this photograph. What realities does the photo convey?

6. *Photobooth.* Photos collected by Babbette Hines.

   The photobooth was created in 1925 by a Siberian immigrant named Anatol Josepho and was marketed as a way to make photography available to the masses. The device was an instant success and has remained popular to this day, inspiring and allowing us to carefully construct images of ourselves. As we can see from the three photographs of children in the sampling of photobooth pictures shown here, only when we become conscious of our ability to create a reality in our recorded image does the photostrip take on the varied and posed look we associate with the photobooth. How do the sitter's gaze and expression affect the way we perceive his or her presentation?

6 picturing argument

Filled with examples, this chapter shows students how visual texts make arguments, with and without the help of words. The end of the introduction to this chapter includes several helpful checklists and questions for students to use when constructing and reading visual arguments. You may want to refer back to these lists often as students go through the assignments accompanying the readings.

Snapshot

This exercise on page 396 asks students to focus on the arguments made by the photos of houses or land in real estate ads. Bring in some ads; you can find some online sources at <www.picturingtexts.com>. Ask students to examine these images and to discuss what the arguments might be. For instance, an ad for a penthouse in a city might appeal to an active businessperson. How does the image appeal to such a person?

ELAINE REICHEK, *Red Delicious*

Reichek's text inserts parts of screen shots of old movies into this photocollage to argue that artistic representations of Native Americans as "others" are problematic.

Focus.

1. This exercise asks students to discuss the argument made by Reichek's photocollage. To help them think about the representation of Native Americans in the film cells surrounding the central figure, discuss them one by one before looking at what they say together. Refer to Reichek's own statement about the text and ask students what the film clips contribute to her argument.

2. This exercise asks students to explore why photocollage might work better as a medium for a visual argument than would a single photograph. You may want to approach this assignment by framing the woman who is the central figure in *Red Delicious* and asking students how they interpret the photo when only the woman is shown. This helps represent what a single photo might try to accomplish versus a photocollage with the other elements in the movie bubbles above her head. Add the movie bubbles back to the picture—or show them alone, without the woman—and ask students to analyze each film cell. Combining all of these elements, ask students what the old film cells add to the message.

3. Ask students to discuss the differences between photocollage and photography. You may also want to discuss with students how they think photocollage differs from digital image manipulation. Is one more "ethical" than the other? Is it valid to ask questions of ethics about art?

Respond.

1. This assignment is to write an essay that describes *Red Delicious* and analyzes Reichek's argument. Are they persuaded by her argument? Does her photocollage help them to take a new perspective on Native Americans? How does her photocollage work to persuade them? Have students refer to the questions at the beginning of this chapter to help them analyze her argument.

2. This assignment asks students to create their own photocollage as a visual argument. If they have trouble coming up with a coherent design

idea, ask them to jot down the argument they want to make. You and your students can workshop these ideas, offering suggestions such as what pictures (and words) might represent the ideas they want to portray.

3. This assignment asks students to workshop and review photocollages they created for the previous question. This is a good opportunity for students to analyze each others' texts. Try hanging all the photocollages around the room so students can look at each one. You might want to make multiple copies of the visual argument questions given in this chapter and have each student write a short analysis of one collage. The students can use these responses to revise their work.

JESSE LEVINE, "Turnabout Map"

This is a good example of how a visual text makes an argument, showing a map that appears to be upside down, at least to North American eyes. Levine's design asks audiences to be aware of or to rethink their worldviews.

Focus.

1. This question asks students to draw upon their historical and cultural understandings of the United States' relationship to South America during the early 1980s. If students do not have this information, you can approach this assignment in several ways: a. have students research the time period to see how and why Levine may have designed the map as he did; b. research this topic and give students a short description of these events; or c. have students analyze the map and hypothesize why the map is situated as it is.

2. A good way to approach this question is to have students discuss whether they have seen any other maps that changed their traditional reference points. For instance, maps created in Russia show North America to be very small and on the opposite side of the map from where Americans are used to seeing it. If possible, bring in an example of such a map (or assign students to find one). Have them find and

read a non-Western map to see if they can even locate places they know. How different are these maps from the ones they are used to seeing? How does Levine's map relate to these?

3. In this discussion, students can offer their analyses of how effective Levine's map is. What was their initial reaction? How did they first begin to understand its meaning? Do they believe Levine's purpose—to reorient our ways of seeing and understanding the North American perspective of the world—is effectively carried out?

Respond.

1. This project asks students to create a map that reorients a region that is in conflict. This assignment might best be accomplished by starting a class discussion about areas of the world that are in conflict. Have students brainstorm about what they know or do some research to come up with areas they might include in their maps. They can trace the regions from another map. If you do this assignment in class, it would help to bring books with maps in them, colored paper, pencils, glue, scissors, transparencies, and tracing paper.

2. In this assignment, students will re-create a map of an area they know well, to include (argue for) certain details. You may want to bring in a map to analyze in class, pointing out what features are included and what are left off. For example, a map might be geared specifically to adventure-loving tourists and only include waterfalls, hiking locations, and campsites. Or it may include only four-star hotels and restaurants. Have students create a list of missing elements they would want to include on their maps. Perhaps students will want to individually re-create the map they analyzed as a class, each for a different purpose.

3. This assignment asks students to create a map of their state, as they believe it should be represented. They may want to decide on some design principles before starting. For instance, do they want it to look traditional, with colors designating certain spots, or would they prefer a cartoonish, hand-drawn map (which might be easier for them to pro-

duce)? Will they have a common legend, or will they draw what each object they want to represent looks like on the map. Have students refer to the maps in Chapter 1 for examples.

MICHAELA SULLIVAN, *King Leopold's Ghost*

This reading is of the book cover of *King Leopold's Ghost*, which was made by overlaying several images to make the argument that King Leopold of Belgium created havoc in the Congo when he colonized it.

Focus.

1. This question asks students to consider what the juxtaposition between the image of the Congolese children with Leopold's state portrait argues. How might students react to seeing only children on the cover? What other texts might the visual remind them of? What if they saw only Leopold's image on the cover? What are the differences in power between these two images? How do they work together to create a completely different meaning than they could individually?

2. You could use the cover of *Picturing Texts* for this discussion. There is a note about the cover design on the inside cover, which you could use to start discussion. It might be interesting to compare it with another composition reader—to compare the tone of the two books—and then discuss how the type, color, title, image, finish, and even trim size affect the tone.

3. One way to approach this question is to ask students to think about the phrase "Never judge a book by its cover." What do they think this means? Is it always accurate? Then, have students look at the covers in the textbook and answer the questions for this assignment. After they determine the answers for each of these, have them revisit the question of judging books by their covers. Is this adage true?

Respond.

1. This assignment asks students to analyze two cover designs for the same book. Ask them to classify the genre of visual texts on each cover. What does the use of stock photos convey? What does the use of line-art illustrations convey? What do students think is the context for line-art drawings such as those shown? Is the way they are used in this context similar or different to how students might expect them to be used?

2. This assignment asks students to design a cover for their favorite book. In doing so, they will need to consider the rhetorical choices of audience and purpose. If students have access to page layout or image programs such as Adobe's publishing suite Pagemaker, InDesign, and Photoshop, they may use these to create a digital version of their texts. Alternatively, any word-processing program such as Word or WordPerfect will allow them to work with graphics and words to create their cover. Or, they can cut and paste images and words onto paper or a transparency. Remind students that a book's cover should make audiences aware of the subject matter of the book, even if metaphorically.

3. This assignment asks students to write a justification of their book cover designs. Refer them to the questions in the introduction of this chapter if they need help evaluating and arguing on behalf of their particular designs.

Richard Misrach and Jason Berry, "Cancer Alley: The Poisoning of the American South"

This reading focuses on how industry has affected the landscape and health of southern Louisiana. Accompanying the essay by Jason Berry is a photo of a polluted river in Louisiana taken by Richard Misrach. This is a good example of how words and images combine to make an argument.

Focus.

1. For this discussion, you may want to help students picture the Mississippi River by reading a passage from Mark Twain's *Life on the Mississippi*. Visit <www.picturingtexts.com> for links to sample passages. After reading the passage, asks students how they picture the Mississippi to which Twain refers. Make a list on the board of all the adjectives they use and perhaps of all the nouns and adjectives Twain uses. To compare Twain's world to Berry's current portrayal of the Mississippi, ask students to list some of the images Berry uses in his article. How do the two lists compare? Because of the contrast, can they surmise why Berry started the essay with the Twain quote?

2. Students may want to analyze visually the composition of this photo as a way to discuss how Misrach's picture is both beautiful and tragic— and what argument the photo alone makes.

3. For this assignment, tell students to underline each reference to the "look" of the river and countryside as they read through the essay. Write a list on the board of the major descriptions of pollution and see how many there are. Compare these descriptions to the picture that accompanies the article. You may want to have students write a passage that describes what the photo shows, to see how Berry's argument would have to proceed if the pictures were not there.

Respond.

1. Students will need to analyze the compositional elements of the two photos for this assignment. Ask students to write about the argument each photo makes—how does each photo juxtapose nature with other subjects to make a statement? If they need help getting started, have them list all of the objects in each photo and then compare those lists.

2. This assignment asks students to explore their local area for signs of change in the landscape. After reading the Berry article, students might be interested in industrial wastelands, but you might also encourage them to look for other signs of change. Perhaps they know about a

farm that has been in operation for decades, amidst a changing land-scape. Or the rejuvenation of a downtown shopping district. There are lots of options. You may want to come up with a list of some options before class, so students who need help with a topic have a few to choose from. This assignment might also be a great way for them to do research at their school or local library, to interview people who might know about the history of the area, or to find archives about the site.

You may want students to focus on a small section of the area. Assign students to small groups to study certain locations. An additional ap-proach to this assignment is to have students create a map of the area and a Web site with that map linked to the photo essays the students create.

3. This assignment asks students to create an ad for an environmental is-sue. Have them examine the student example in the textbok to see how it makes its argument through comparison, balance, and unity. Make sure to have them specify an audience for the ad.

SHIRLEY ANN GRAU AND CLARENCE JOHN LAUGHLIN, "Memory, Mint Juleps, and My Grandfather"

This reading highlights Grau's childhood memories of her grandfather telling stories on his front porch and includes a photo by Clarence John Laughlin that helps show readers the setting Grau remembers.

Focus.

1. Begin this exercise by asking students if Laughlin's photo reminds them of anything. Even if they do not know the setting of the photo, their memory of similar images will help them contextualize the decaying mansion. Depending on what part of the country your school is in, stu-dents may have a vastly different memory of estate houses such as the ones pictured in this essay. Prompt students by asking them to think historically about what a large white mansion might represent. What

does the decay, as presented in Laughlin's photo, suggest about those settings?

2. This exercise asks students to examine the argument in the Laughlin and Misrach photos. They should focus on what the photos say about place. You might bring in a photo or transparency of a large white house (maybe a representation of a southern plantation, like the one in Laughlin's photo) and have students discuss what contextual clues help them make meaning for this kind of text. Next, show a photo of an overgrown tree (like the weeping willow in Laughlin's photo) and have students discuss its meaning. If you're working with transparencies, overlay the tree onto the house, as Laughlin has done, and discuss what these two juxtaposed elements argue.

3. For this question, you may want to ask students whether Laughlin's photos, accompanied by Grau's story, intend to make us happy or sad. Do they accomplish both? Ask students how Laughlin's picture helps them to read and understand Grau's story. Ask them to imagine that they had not seen the picture before reading the story. Given the details of Grau's narrative, where would they think the story takes place? Does the photo match the setting they imagine, help clarify it, or differ from it altogether? What does the photo add to the argument?

Respond.

1. This assignment asks students to think about how photos can do more than record—how, for instance, they might be poetic interpretations. You might want to start by having students talk about the metaphors in Laughlin's photo, such as what the tree might represent, or what the house means. What does the juxtaposition of the two mean? Have students draw on their knowledge about such objects to help them see the metaphors created by these images.

2. For this assignment, students are asked to envision how they would like to see a place they know. Instead of asking them to get photos of this place (which may be difficult if the place is not close by), have

them draw or create a photocollage of how they want the area to look. Then have them write about the elements that would need to change for the place to become what they would like.

Picture This

This assignment asks students to analyze the visual argument of holiday cards and then to create their own greeting card. Ask students how they would represent their own families and cultures in a holiday greeting. The examples shown are Christmas and New Year's cards, but of course other holidays might be important to students—Valentine's Day, Veterans Day, and so on. How might the greeting—and the argument—differ from the ones shown here? Is a picture the most important element, or do words matter more? What wording might best represent the card's occasion—and its argument?

Context and Questions for the Gallery of Images

1. *Fragile.* Photo by Neil Ryder Hoos, 1993.
   Hoos looks for narratives in posters and ads, billboards, and other such public texts. He photographs his images with an editorial eye, often juxtaposing many layers of text to emphasize what he wishes the image to convey. This photo pairs a heart-shaped candy box with the words from a packing box. As a photograph, it projects one meaning—but we change it from a snapshot to be a valentine, and it makes a different argument. What various arguments does the image make? Do you think the materials the objects are made of add any meaning?

2. *The U.S.A. as Seen from Canada.* World Eagle.
   Most maps position nations north–south, assuming the North Pole to be at the top and the South Pole at the bottom. This map shows what happens when you reverse that perspective, looking at the United States south from Canada. The map was created by World Eagle, a non-profit publisher that specializes in comparative data, maps, and graphs. What argument do you think this map makes?

3. *Toyota Corolla Ad.* Designed by Saatchi and Saatchi, 1997.

   This ad appeals to parents concerned for the safety of their children. The ad is unusual in attempting to make an abstract, invisible concept—safety—visible and in not showing the car it is trying to sell. How would the argument change if we were to substitute the sign from the image on p. 424 for the bubblewrap? Which argument would be stronger? More effective? Why?

4. *Does This Hurt?* Ad for the Chiropractic Association of South Africa.

   This ad asks a simple question, and by positioning type sideways it also leads readers to the answer. How do the simplicity and directness of the image and layout make this an effective argument? What is the argument here?

5. *Untitled.* School, Cumberland Mountain Farms, near Scottsboro, Alabama.

   Photo by Carl Mydans, 1936, taken for the FSA. What argument does this photo make? You might have students try composing a title for the image—and then thinking about how their title reflects (affects?) the argument.

6. *Untitled.* Son of a tenant farmer, Greensboro, Alabama.

   Photo by Jack Delano, 1941, taken for the FSA. What argument does this photo make about tenant farming? How does its composition affect that argument? How would it be different if the boy were looking at the camera rather than away?

7. *Fred Astaire Dance Studio Ad.* By Kohnke Hanneken Ad Agency, Milwaukee.

   This ad argues that even the mundane task of taking out the garbage can be fun when you know how to dance. How does the perspective in this photo contribute to the ad's effectiveness?

8. *UNICEF Ad.*

   This ad against child labor makes a convincing argument by putting the child laborer on the label of the jeans that he is making. What details tell us that he is too young to be sewing pants? How does the close-up view of the jeans and label add to the argument?

7 designing texts

This chapter focuses on design and how it affects the message of a text, discussing the design elements that students need to learn: typography, layout, images, and other graphics. Most important, it shows them how to think about design and images rhetorically, as a means of communication rather than as mere decoration. The chapter also provides guidelines for evaluating designs for their rhetorical effectiveness; see the helpful chart on pages 462–63.

Snapshot

This exercise asks students to think about how cropping a photo can change what it shows and what it means. Have them photocopy a snapshot and crop it three different ways and then think (or write) about the different texts that result.

PAULA SCHER, "The Palm Beach County Ballot"

This reading shows the infamous Palm Beach ballot of the 2000 presidential election, annotated by a professional designer to show the many design flaws. We now know all too well how this badly designed ballot confused voters; this reading provides a good opportunity to discuss the importance of keeping an audience in mind when designing a text.

Focus.

1. This question asks students to look at how the order in which the candidates were listed implied a certain hierarchy. This is a good exercise to get them thinking about Western reading habits and our patterns of reading top to bottom and left to right. Make an overhead of this ballot and draw or point out poorly designed areas.

2. This question is a follow-up to the previous one, asking students to examine how this ballot might be ineffectively designed for English-speaking readers. Ask them what elements do not read from left to right (the entire right column, for instance).

Respond.

1. This question asks students to focus on all the elements of the ballot design and how they might signal that the designer of the ballot is Republican. Although the students will not be able to determine party affiliation based only on the composition (placing Republican candidates in the most prominent spot could, after all, be just a poor decision made by someone not trained to know that the upper-left corner is the first place readers look), this is a good question for discussing what knowledge designers need to create texts that are fair and impartial.

2. This question asks students to explore the differences between the Palm Beach ballot and several ballots from other countries, including some with photos and symbols. Would including photos and symbols be an effective strategy in the United States?

3. This assignment invites students to design their own ballot. Because you have probably spent some time discussing the Palm Beach ballot, you may want students to try redesigning it. Have them work in groups so that they can decide together what design strategies might work better than others. After they have designed their ballots, have them review the ballots with another group to see how effective their design choices were. They can use those responses in their essays to reflect on

how their ideas about the effectiveness of designs were similar to or different from their classmates' ideas.

Sarah Boxer, "A New Poland, No Joke"

This text discusses the redesign of Poland's tourism logo and whether or not that design is effective.

Focus.

1. This exercise asks students to reflect on the connotations of kites and eagles and to consider whether their own experiences with these images match those behind the redesign of Poland's logo. You might have students discuss the politically charged nature of the eagle as a country's symbol. Bring several examples of the eagle on governmental paraphernalia, such as on the U.S. quarter, dollar bill, or seal, or Russia's double-headed eagle. Based on what they know about each country's history, why do students think Poland would not want to use the eagle as its symbol?

2. This exercise asks students to consider further how symbols such as the eagle take on the meanings of the products or countries they label. Bring in several examples of logos—the Nike Swoosh, the McDonald's Golden Arches, the Macintosh Apple—and ask students to identify these logos and discuss how they know what they are. (Likely, they may not be able to articulate where or how they know these symbols, since they have become so pervasive.) For an addition to this exercise, bring in some examples of spoof ads—or have students review the Adbusters-affiliated Web site, UnBrand America (see <www.picturingtexts.com>) and discuss the purpose of such a campaign.

Respond.

1. This assignment asks students to think about what "branding" means when applied to a country. Have them reflect on how they choose to represent themselves and decide whether the symbols of their country apply to them. Do they want to be represented by the eagle, the American flag, the melting pot, or McDonald's? Do they think these symbols of the United States accurately portray this country? What experiences support their attitude toward their country's symbols?

2. This assignment asks students to think about and create an appropriate and positive branding for something with which they are familiar. Suggest to students that they brand *themselves* (many designers are asked to do this to get jobs). Have them start by making a list of all the traits they would want others to know about them. For homework (or in class, if an Internet connection is available), have them search for clip art or other graphics that might help visually to explain these traits and combine these graphics, with words if needed, to produce their personal logos. Have students write a short justification for why they chose these texts to represent themselves, explaining who the audience for their brand is, why they chose the images they did, and what they intend to represent about themselves with their brand.

3. After analyzing the brands above and creating their own brand, students will analyze the Sydney poster. If they are not familiar with the landmarks shown in the poster, have them do some research so they can better understand why this poster may or may not reflect the image of Sydney that Australians want to portray.

Tibor Kalman, "What's Happening to Logos?"

This reading questions the purpose and usefulness of company logos and the effectiveness of their designs.

Focus.

1. This question asks students to think about how the design of the text contributes to its argument. Refer students back to the chapter introduction to read about how typography helps readers get some sense of a text's purpose.

2. This exercise asks students why Kalman used a flow chart to show a bunch of logos. Point out that flow charts are typically used in corporations or businesses to show processes. Have them examine the written text in the chart—does it strike the kind of tone they would expect in a flow chart? If not, how would they characterize the tone, and how does it contribute to Kalman's argument?

Respond.

1. For this assignment, you may want to group students and have each group look up and define "logo," "logos," and "logogram," and perhaps present the information to the class. Ask them to discuss the main ideas they found, including the original appearance of the word, a summary of how the meaning changed (or did not change) over time, and a comparison of the meanings.

2. One way to approach this assignment is to have students sit in one spot for half an hour and keep a list of all the logos they see on people or things that pass by. In class, have them discuss how many logos for the same company they saw, what a lack of familiar logos might mean, and what the prominence of certain logos suggests about the consumer habits of the area.

3. This assignment asks students to examine how typefaces can be used to brand national magazines. They will need to compare the typefaces of two similar magazines. You may want to supply some examples for them or have them research magazines in the library or bookstore. They will need to analyze the magazines for audience and purpose and determine whether or not the typeface fulfills those rhetorical goals

and then think about whether the typographic differences help distinguish each magazine as a brand.

Ellen Lupton and J. Abbott Miller, "McPaper: *USA Today* and the Journalism of Hope"

This text discusses how the nationwide newspaper *USA Today* started trends of presenting happy news and using color graphics to explain stories (sometimes inaccurately) in order to offer more news in less reading time.

Focus.

1. This question asks students to discuss how their news-gathering experiences differ from their parents' experiences. Have students list all the ways their parents listened to or watched the news when they were growing up. Then have them list how they learned to gather news when they were growing up themselves. Finally, have them compare those lists to a list of how they get news now.

2. One way to approach this assignment is to have students rewrite a news story they find in the local paper so that it describes all the necessary information in a way that mimics the "happy" style of *USA Today*. Ask them to analyze their word choice to see which parts of speech they have to change to make the story happier—does a happy news story depend more on nouns, verbs, or adjectives, or all of them? Have them also redesign a graphic to see if they can create a happier but still effective version.

Respond.

1. For this assignment, you may want to bring in (or have students research and bring to class) examples of some newspapers from 1982, the year *USA Today* first appeared. How do the front pages of three

papers—say, the *Wall Street Journal*, the *New York Times*, and *USA Today*—compare? Similarly, have students find examples of online newspapers and see how they are designed compared with the front pages of their print counterparts. How have the designs of papers changed (or not) over the last few decades? Has the presentation changed the way the front pages look in *both* online and print forms? After considering these questions, students can begin writing a rhetorical analysis of the newspapers.

2. This assignment asks students to analyze rhetorically a visual and verbal text from *USA Today*. You can direct them to print or online versions. Whichever they pick, encourage them to examine how one version might present information differently from another or have them analyze the same article in both mediums and write about the differences. For example, the print version of a story might contain a photograph or a chart while the online version might contain an interactive graphic and the layout might be different to take advantage of the screen size.

JIM HEIMANN, "May I Take Your Order?"

This text shows restaurant menu designs spanning several decades. It speaks to how restaurants use design to appeal to customers.

Focus.

1. Start this question by asking students what the font on the cover of Heimann's book reminds them of. This might help them determine what kind of restaurant and/or era the font represents. You may want students to do a Web search on "fonts" and another keyword they think the font on the cover represents, such as "deco," "1950s," or "script." See how many fonts they can find that fall under similar categories. Have them print out a page with the fonts they find and compare them in class, describing what era each font was used in or what kind of restaurant the fonts imply.

2. This question asks students to think about the purpose of the mock menu disclaimer at the bottom of the contents page. What does it tell them about the book and its purposes?

Respond.

1. For this assignment, bring in a listing of restaurants grouped into categories. For instance, the Yellow Pages often lists restaurants by kind of cuisine. If possible, collect menus from restaurants the students are unlikely to have eaten at, such as four-star restaurants. Having a wide range of menus will help; some restaurant owners do not mind lending menus if they know they will be returned.

   Once students have collected menus (advise them that many restaurants have take-out menus they can ask for), have them categorize the menus in some way—by cuisine, price, dine-in/take-out, and so forth. Do they notice any similarities in design within each group? across groups? For instance, a dine-in menu from a Chinese restaurant might have color pictures or longer descriptions of the food, while the take-out menu might only list the names of dishes. They can use these comparisons to write their analysis of the menus. Encourage students to choose menus, if feasible, from restaurants they want to patronize (this will help with the next assignment, when they will be asked to design their own menu).

2. In this assignment, students will design their own menus. Start by asking them to think about what they like and do not like on the menus they have analyzed. These will be some starting points for designing a menu for an imaginary restaurant or redesigning the menu for a restaurant they like.

3. This assignment asks students to design a matchbook cover that functions as an anti-smoking ad. Have them consider the color of the cover as well as the typeface and the information they will give (do they want to make up a company or restaurant name that plays on the idea of smoking or just use a declarative phrase?). Have them also consider what graphics they could include that would help persuade a smoking audience to quit.

Picture This

This assignment brings together all of the design elements students have studied and practiced in the readings for this chapter. They will write and design a film review, imitating a newspaper layout, including a headline and images that represent the film. They will also design a poster that advertises the film, which might include the film's logo or some representation of that logo. In completing this assignment, students will practice their writing and design for several print media.

To start on this assignment, have students review the genre features of the texts they will produce. How large are headlines? What fonts are used? How many columns of text are in a newspaper review? What size typeface is necessary for a poster to be seen? What colors? Have them decide which features they think work best and use those in their own designs. When students are finished, have them present their designs in class to get responses about which design elements resulted in the most effective communication.

Context and Questions for the Gallery of Images

1. *Bring in Da Noise, Bring in Da Funk.* Poster design by Paula Scher of Pentagram Design.
   Scher is known for her great ability to illustrate and convey emotion with type. "Letter-forms have character," she once said. "Letter-forms have weight, so designing with typography is like creating a montage. You're putting elements together in a specific way that creates a certain dynamic, and the words themselves help illustrate the point. You're using scale, color, texture to create an impression. . . . If I'm doing a poster for a play, I've got to convey the spirit of the show and a sense of what the play is about. Part of design is creating order, and some of design is evoking spirit." What "certain dynamic" does this poster have? What spirit does it evoke, and how does Scher's use of scale, color, and type convey that spirit?

2. *Ad for Hewitt Associates.*
   Typography is used here to represent both the figures in the image and their thoughts. The figures in this ad are made up of type; in the poster

on the facing page, the background is made up of type. Note the difference between the two. What if this ad had photos of actual lab workers. How then could their thoughts be shown—in a bubble? a caption? a heading? Try writing one of these, and compare it with this ad. What does the typography here convey that a caption or other form cannot—and vice versa?

3. *Swiss Highways Poster*. From the Design Museum in Zurich.
   What do you think the design of this poster says about the museum? How else could that message be said?

4. *Preamble*. By Mike Wilkens, 1987.
   The artist assembled actual license plates with typography which present the preamble to the U.S. Constitution. What do you think this composition says about the Constitution? about vanity license plates?

5. *Photoessay*. By Eugene Smith, 1959.
   In 1955 the photographer Eugene Smith was commissioned to spend three weeks taking photographs for a book commemorating the bicentennial of Pittsburgh. He stayed a year and took seventeen thousand photographs. Only a small number of the photographs were ever used. In 1959, *Popular Photography* magazine gave Smith the opportunity to reproduce some of these photographs and also gave him the rare opportunity to create his own layouts. It allows us to see into the vision he had when taking the images. In later years, Smith often returned to this version of his Pittsburgh work as an example of his "many layered" approach to editing. Of the opening picture of the steelworker, which happened to be one of the last photos he made in Pittsburgh, Smith said, "I needed a picture of man submerged underneath industry, but not lost." The following is part of the essay that was published in *Popular Photography*. In this essay, Smith tells a story about Pittsburgh— the story he discovered while taking the pictures. What story does this essay tell? You probably cannot read all the words, but how important are Smith's words to the story? What about the layout—what does it add to the message?